D. Caroline C

Greyhounds

Everything about Adoption, Purchase, Care,
Nutrition, Behavior, and Training

With 49 Color Photographs
Illustrations by Tana Hakanson

BARRON'S

Acknowledgments

The information contained in this book comes from a variety of sources: breeders, original research, scientific articles, veterinary journals, and a library of dog books. But by far my most heartfelt gratitude must go to my most demanding teachers, who have taught me the skills of both home repair and dog repair, allowed ample testing opportunities for behavioral problem cures, and whetted my curiosity (and carpets) about everything canine for the past 20 years: Baha, Khyber, Tundra, Kara, Hypatia, Savannah, Sissy, Dixie, Bobby, Kitty, Jeepers, Bean-Boy, Junior, Khyzi, Wolfman, Stinky, Honey, and Luna.

All inquiries should be addressed to:
Barron's Educational Series, Inc.
250 Wireless Boulevard
Hauppauge, NY 11788

International Standard Book No. 0-8120-9314-3

Library of Congress Catalog Card No. 95-49004

Library of Congress Cataloging-in-Publication Data
Coile, D. Caroline.
    Greyhounds : everything about adoption,
    purchase, care, nutrition, behavior, and training /
    D. Caroline Coile ; drawings by Tana Hakanson
        p.   cm. — (A Complete pet owner's manual)
    Includes bibliographical references and index.
    ISBN 0-8120-9314-3
    1. Greyhounds. I. Title. II. Series.
SF429.G8C635   1996
636.7′53—dc20   95-49004
                                                    CIP

Printed in Hong Kong

15 14 13 12 11 10 9 8 7 6 5 4 3

About the Author

Caroline Coile is an award-winning author who has written articles about dogs for both scientific and lay publications. She holds a Ph.D. in the field of neuroscience and behavior, with special interests in canine sensory systems, genetics, and behavior. A sighthound owner since 1963, her own dogs have been nationally ranked in conformation, obedience, and field-trial competition.

Photo Credits

Toni Tucker: front cover, page 17; Barbara Augello: inside front cover, page 4, inside back cover; Susan Green: pages 21 bottom, 24, 32, 33, 36, 52, 80, 92 top, back cover; Bonnie Nance: pages 16, 21 top, 41, 53 top, 68, 101; Judith Strom: pages 13, 28, 40 top and bottom, 56, 64, 92 bottom; Michelle Earle-Bridges: page 14; Paul Luna: pages 5, 20, 93; Dale Jackson, Ph.D.: pages 9, 37, 49, 60, 73, 100 bottom; Val Cullen: page 8 top, 45, 53 bottom, 69, 85; Diana Coile: page 8 bottom, 96 top and bottom; Bart Mackey: page 29; Georg Bower: pages 48, 88; Robert Nix: pages 72, 89; Melony Cleveland: page 100 top; Chris Smoot: page 97; Katherine Crawford: pages 81, 84.

Important Note

This pet owner's guide tells the reader how to buy or adopt, and care for a Greyhound. The author and the publisher consider it important to point out that the advice given in the book is meant primarily for normally developed dogs of excellent physical health and good character.

Anyone who adopts a fully grown dog should be aware that the animal has already formed its basic impressions of human beings. The new owner should watch the animal carefully, including its behavior toward humans, and should meet the previous owner. If the dog being adopted is a former racer it is important to see how the dog was treated by the former owner and trainer. If the dog comes from a shelter, it may be possible to get some information on the dog's background and peculiarities there. There are dogs that, as a result of bad experiences with humans, behave in an unnatural manner or may even bite. Only people that have experience with dogs should take in such animals.

Caution is further advised in the association of children with dogs, in meeting with other dogs, and in exercising the dog without a leash.

Even well-behaved and carefully supervised dogs sometimes do damage to someone else's property or cause accidents. It is therefore in the owner's interest to be adequately insured against such eventualities, and we strongly urge all dog owners to purchase a liability policy that covers their dog.

Contents

Preface 4

The Noblest Beast 6
The Ancient Greyhound 6
Through the Centuries 7
Two Halves of One Breed 8
The Greyhound in Trouble 10

**Understanding the Racing
Greyhound 12**
Life on the Farm 12
Training for the Track 13
Win, Place, Show . . . or Go 13
Fate of the Retired Racer 15

Greyhound Choices 17
The AKC versus the NGA
   Greyhound 17
Locating an NGA Greyhound 18
Locating an AKC Greyhound 18
Why You Can't Breed Your
   Greyhound 19
The Reality Check 19
The Greyhound as a Pet 20

Welcoming Your Greyhound 23
Greyhound Essentials 23
Housing 25
Safeguarding Your Greyhound 26
Safeguarding Your Home 28
The Homecoming 28

Life With a Greyhound 31
Just Say "No" 31
Housebreaking 31
Greyhounds and Other Pets 32
Weather Extremes 33
HOW-TO: Understanding Your
   Greyhound 34
The Greyhound Abroad 37
Boarding 38
Greyhound at Large 39

Greyhound Nutrition 41
The Galloping Gourmet 42
Keeping Your Greyhound Trim 44
A Note on Bloat 45

Greyhound Maintenance 46
Coat and Skin Care 46
Nail Care 50
Ear Care 51
Dental Care 52
The Health Check 54
The Senior Greyhound 54

In Sickness and in Health 57
Greyhound Physiology Is Different 57
Choosing Your Veterinarian 59
Preventive Medicine 59
Common Ailments and Symptoms 61
HOW-TO: Dealing With
   Emergencies 62

Greyhound Fitness 67
Conditioning 67
Safety Afield 69
HOW-TO: Dealing With Running
   Injuries 70
Coursing, of Course 74

To Train a Greyhound 78
What Every Good Greyhound Trainer
  Should Know 78
Dress for Success 81
HOW-TO: Solving Behavior
  Problems 82
What Every Good Greyhound Should
  Know 84
Higher Education 87

Fun With Greyhounds 89
Mind Games 89
Obedience Trials 90
The Greyhound Good Citizen 91
Tracking 91
Agility 91

The Show Greyhound 93
The AKC Greyhound Standard 93
Showing a Greyhound 96

The Greyhound Companion 98
Sharing Your Greyhound 98
For Better or Worse 98
Till Death Do Us Part 98

Useful Addresses and Literature 101

Index 103

Preface

The world's fastest couch potato, the greyhound is today finding its way into more homes and hearts than ever before in its long history. With the most distinctive silhouette in dogdom, the greyhound's form has been immortalized from the tombs of ancient Egypt to the buses of modern America. Yet few people really know the greyhound, and few have a chance to get to know it before they walk away from the track with a full-grown adopted ex-racer in one hand and an instruction sheet in the other.

Because of its unique physical and behavioral traits, the greyhound has health and safety requirements not shared by any other breed. Greyhound veterinary and conditioning texts address these needs but are not generally available to the public, nor do they consider the lifestyle of the pet greyhound. This book was written to fill that gap, and is intended as a concise owner's manual for the greyhound at home.

With its almost feline qualities, the greyhound has quickly won lifelong devotees that would now never consider another breed. But precisely because it is not the prototypical dog, others who expected more doglike traits have been disappointed. This is your invitation to meet the greyhound before inviting one into your home.

The greyhound's future depends upon people who are not content to admire it from afar, but insist on embracing it into their family. And that depends on just giving it a chance to become your fastest of friends, because beneath the noble exterior is a heart racing with love.

D. Caroline Coile, Ph.D.

Among the most specialized and beautiful of canids, the greyhound is the ultimate running machine.

The Noblest Beast

Unleashed, her flight begins. Soaring in leaps and bounds, she outstrips the wind, until, with sides heaving she returns to her master, who too has soared through the eyes of the greyhound. No matter that the quarry was not caught, or indeed, that there was anything but the horizon to chase–sharing this quiet time, punctuated only by the cadence of pounding feet, is what binds greyhound and human. It has been thus throughout the ages.

The Ancient Greyhound

In the year 124 A.D., the Greek historian Arrian wrote of hunting with greyhounds:

"The true sportsman does not take out his dogs to destroy the Hares, but for the sake of the course, and the contest between the dogs and the Hares, and is glad if the Hare escapes."

Yet the greyhound's roots reach even further into antiquity, to a time when the human unleashed the dog not for sport, but to provide meat for sustenance. The wide expanses of North Africa and Arabia provided a land where speed reigned. A dog that

Dogs of unmistakable greyhound form were often depicted on ancient art forms. This pack of hounds was depicted on the Egyptian tomb of Rekh-me-Re, circa 1450 BC.

could overtake fleeing game and bring it back to share with its human pack members was a valuable animal, and the discriminating breeding of such animals tended to reproduce fleetness. Thus, one of the first specialized types of dogs to be selectively bred was the greyhound. Since time immemorial it has been one of the most consistently bred and revered forms of domesticated animals.

Dogs of undeniable greyhound form are depicted on the tombs of ancient Pharaohs over 4,000 years ago. The beauty of the greyhound, one of four things "comely in going" was (according to some translations from the Hebrew) recorded by Solomon in Proverbs (30: 29–31). Yet the ancient greyhound was not the greyhound as we know it today.

Dogs of the Pharaohs were more like the saluki, a Middle-Eastern greyhoundlike breed. The saluki was a dog of the nomad, and as such would have traveled throughout the desert lands. Although it was so revered that it was never sold, it was on occasion presented as a gift to an esteemed visitor. No doubt salukis (also called Persian greyhounds) were presented to the caravan traders, and through them were introduced even farther throughout the world. The desert greyhounds eventually found themselves in Babylon, Afghanistan, Russia, Turkistan, Greece, Rome, Gaul, and Britain. Different subtypes developed to adapt to the various climates, terrain, and game in these different locales. The greyhounds of the colder climates were crossed with other native breeds to achieve thicker coats. Thus there came to be a family of related dogs having in common a sleek build and the ability to hunt game by sight, a family now known as the sighthounds. The quintessential sighthound is the greyhound.

Through the Centuries

The sighthounds of Greece, Rome, and later, Britain seemed to most resemble the modern greyhound, and today's greyhound descends mostly from the British form. By Saxon times greyhounds were well established in Britain and were valued both by commoners for their ability to feed the family and by nobility for the sport of the chase.

The year 1014 marked the beginning of an ignoble four-century chapter in greyhound history: the enactment of the Forest Laws. Serfs and slaves were prohibited from greyhound ownership, and greyhounds owned by freemen living near the royal forests had to be lamed, either by chopping three toes off a front paw or by severing ligaments in the knee. This mutilation was to prevent a commoner from attempting to hunt game for food at the expense of royal sport.

Even after the Forest Laws were repealed, greyhounds remained dogs of the nobility. With the growing importance of agriculture and domestic animals for food, the reliance of commoners on greyhounds for sustenance had been greatly reduced. Coursing—the pursuit of game by sighthounds—was increasingly for sport among both nobles and commoners. Elizabeth I, a coursing enthusiast, decreed that rules be set forth by which dogs could be fairly judged, thus setting the stage for the "sport of queens." In 1776 the first coursing club was formed, and during the 1800s coursing became an important pastime for the upper class.

Are Greyhounds Gray?

Some greyhounds are gray, and many people assume that's how the breed got its name. But the name more likely comes from another source. Some believed it is derived from "gazehound," which was in turn either another name for sighthound or was derived from gazelle hound, another term for the saluki. Or it may come from "Graius," meaning Greek, or from the Latin "gradus," referring to its foremost grade in dogdom. Of course, many present-day greyhound owners would assert that it is simply because greyhounds are "great hounds"!

In the late 1700s Lord Orford, an enthusiastic if eccentric coursing devotee, set about to improve greyhounds by crossing them with other breeds. One of the least likely crosses had to be that with the bulldog (which at that time resembled more the bull terrier of today). Amid the contempt and ridicule of his competitors, Lord Orford bred this cross back to greyhounds for seven generations. Then, to the further shock of his competitors, he took his best crossbreed to the coursing field and promptly won every course. Simply put, the hybrid "Czarina" could not be beaten. Still Lord Orford's fellow coursing enthusiasts refused to touch the bulldog blood. Only after Czarina's grandsons, Snowball and Major, proved themselves to be similarly invincible was the new blood accepted. It can be said that every present day greyhound traces back to these two dogs.

Greyhounds had also made their way to America, having accompanied the Spanish in their expeditions of the early 1500s. It was not uncommon for early European explorers to include a greyhound among the dogs that accompanied them across country,

With a heritage tracing to the Pharaohs, today's greyhound is remarkably unchanged through the centuries.

This gray AKC champion greyhound is in the minority in the show ring as far as color is concerned.

and a greyhound was even a well-known figure at Valley Forge during the Revolutionary War. But only when the settlers began to farm the Midwest did the greyhound arrive en masse. As crops were overrun with jackrabbits, European immigrants naturally recalled the coursing prowess of greyhounds and had them brought from Europe for vermin control. Again sport grew from necessity, and the coursing of jackrabbits, coyotes, and other game on the plains became a popular pastime. General Custer was known to keep a large number of greyhounds, and Teddy Roosevelt also enjoyed hunting with greyhounds.

Two Halves of One Breed

The problem with coursing as a sport was that it was not readily accessible to the masses. Closed park coursing, in which the dogs were let

A century of selection with emphasis on different attributes has resulted in two different greyhounds: the AKC or show type, modeled by the spotted dog, and the NGA or track type, modeled by the dark dog.

loose after a rabbit in an enclosed area, attracted great public attention in England for a while, but soon lost favor. In 1876 the first exhibition of greyhounds chasing a mechanical rabbit was held in England, but was viewed only as a curiosity. It failed, too, in the United States, where it was presented as a side event to horse racing. It was not until the greyhound races were staged at night under artificial lighting that they erupted as an entertainment spectacle. Track racing quickly outpaced coursing in popularity both in Europe and America.

In racing, the emphasis is upon speed, with little attention to the agility and endurance required of a coursing dog. The coursing dogs provided the stock from which the racing dogs were developed, but soon the racing dogs were bred only with each other. In America racing greyhounds are registered with the National Greyhound Association (NGA). The coursing dogs also provided the foundation for

Built for Speed

What makes greyhounds so fast? For one thing, greyhounds have a style of running known as a double-suspension gallop. Most dogs run like a horse: at full speed there is one period (when the feet are all contracted under the body) when all four feet are off the ground. But in greyhounds and other sighthounds there is a second full-suspension phase, which occurs when the feet are fully extended in front of and behind the body. This period of free flight extends the greyhound's stride and speed. The greyhound is able to run like this because of the structure of its back, which is far more supple than that of most dogs. Thus, the extension and contraction of the back also increases the greyhound's stride. But because this running style is extremely tiring, the greyhound cannot keep this speed up for long.

In the 1800s coursing the European hare in the British Isles became so popular a sport that the top greyhounds achieved near celebrity status.

another modern type of greyhound: the show greyhound.

At the turn of the nineteenth century the exhibition of purebred dogs was beginning to catch the sporting interest of many, and greyhounds were among the earliest breeds to be exhibited. Ideally, a dog that was built right would run right, although many of the best coursing dogs were admittedly lacking in looks. Most of the early show winners were prominent coursing dogs, but as judges came to favor dogs with fewer rough edges, those with a layer of fat tended to win out. The sinewy coursing dogs lost and returned to the field, and show greyhounds began to be bred to each other. In the United States these dogs were the foundation stock for today's American Kennel Club (AKC) registered greyhounds.

Which is the true greyhound? Both the NGA and AKC greyhounds have an equal right to lay claim to the title of greyhound. They came initially from the same stock, but represent the results of selection with different priori-

ties. Still, the greyhound of today is nonetheless remarkably unchanged from the greyhound of a thousand years ago.

In many breeds of dogs the goal of the breeder is to change and thus improve the breed. Greyhound breeders have the challenge of preserving this ancient breed, already perfected by thousands of generations of selection. This challenge has fallen to the breeders of the show-type greyhound, and the best of them are striving to produce greyhounds that are athletic, intelligent, healthy, and beautiful, with the look and coursing ability of the greyhound of antiquity.

The Greyhound in Trouble

For a breed that has been so idolized throughout its long history, the greyhound has seen its share of hard times. But perhaps at no time has the greyhound's future been so tenuous as now. The greyhound is one of the most populous breeds in this country, with thirty thousand to fifty thousand born annually. Its sleek silhouette has long made it a favorite emblem and model for advertising. Everybody knows the greyhound. Yet the AKC ranks the greyhound as one of the least popular of the breeds it recognizes, with fewer than 200 registered annually. And until recently, the sight of a pet greyhound was a rarity.

Why the lack of popularity for the greyhound as pet? Many people have wrongly assumed that greyhounds are not interested in being pets, that all they want to do is run, that they are hyperactive, aggressive, unloving, and unavailable. In fact, those greyhounds that have found their ways into homes are proving those assumptions to be dead wrong. Today many families have discovered that greyhounds make even better pets than they did race dogs, and the adoption of ex-racers has reached unprecedented numbers.

This popularity has come at the expense of the show greyhound, however. Responsible breeders do not breed a litter unless there are homes lined up for puppies, and the instant availability of retired racers has meant that most people wanting a pet greyhound get a greyhound from racing stock, not show stock. There is further concern among show breeders that because the track dogs have not been bred for health or longevity, they bring with them a bevy of hereditary problems previously unheard of in the breed. Although the majority of adoptees are neutered, some remain intact and could be registered with the AKC. If these dogs were bred, show breeders fear that the influx of their genes into the AKC greyhound gene pool could swamp the AKC show greyhound type and introduce hereditary health problems.

Thus, the breed faces the problem of dealing with a constant influx of

The greyhound's double-suspension gallop is more typically cat-like than dog- or horse-like in form. There are two periods when all four feet are off the ground (seen in the rightmost figure of each line), rather than the one period of suspension seen in most breeds.

retired racers, dogs that deserve a chance at home life. But the breed also faces the dilemma that by finding homes for these dogs it seems to condone the overproduction of them in the first place by track breeders and to further curtail breeding of show greyhounds by those who take responsibility for every life they bring into the world.

Understanding the Racing Greyhound

Eight greyhounds parade under the floodlights, their quivering muscles the only clue to their excitement. As the lure begins its journey, the greyhounds howl their frustration at being confined in the starting box, until finally the doors spring open and the dogs bound forward. Their sprint around the track defines single-minded determination, oblivious to the crowd, each other, and even their own injuries. At the end of the race, the eighth-place finisher is as pleased with itself as is the first-place finisher. Unfortunately, its trainer is not.

The trainer has reason to be unhappy if a greyhound runs poorly. The trip around the track is the culmi-nation of a very long and costly journey that began long before that dog was born. It began with the choice of the best possible brood bitch and a substantial stud fee, and continued with optimal prenatal and postnatal care, socialization, handling, and schooling. By the time a pup enters its first race several thousand dollars have already been invested in it. And it has yet to earn a penny back.

Life on the Farm

Most pups begin life inside a nurs-ery room with their dam and litter-mates (average litter size is about seven). After weaning, the litter moves to larger quarters, usually a long run with access to an indoor enclosure.

Early lure training starts as a game, with the pups falling over each other to catch a dragged toy. As they get more keen for the game, they begin to chase and jump in their efforts to snatch the prize.

Some greyhound litters will be sent to a rearing facility at four months of age. By this age the dogs should have received abundant handling and can usually walk on a leash. The pups are put in small groups in a larger paddock so that they can run and cavort with their littermates, building strength and coordination. They may also be allowed access to a large field for unlimited running. Each paddock has a small house for the pups to sleep in.

At 10 to 12 months of age, the grey-hound may once again change homes to live at a training facility. Here its

Greyhound pups love to play with stuffed toys, and often trainers will begin informal training by letting the pups chase after a favorite toy.

formal education starts, beginning with a change to living in a small kennel, or cage. The track greyhound's life is one of routine. The day begins early with the first of three to four paddock "turnouts" of the day. While together each dog wears a kennel muzzle to protect each other from overzealous play.

Training for the Track

Many people assume that greyhounds must be trained to chase live rabbits in order to build some sort of bloodlust for the chase. But two thousand years of breeding has resulted in a dog that is just looking for an excuse to chase something, and this instinct does not need priming with live prey. On the track the dog chases a lure, not a rabbit, and serious training is aimed at encouraging enthusiasm for the lure only. In most states it is illegal for dogs to be trained to chase live animals, but some trainers still believe that they can get an edge by training with live rabbits. Those unethical trainers who are caught doing so are barred from further NGA competition.

Lure enthusiasm is built by tempting the pups with a pole-lure (see page 75) outside of their runs. Yearlings are allowed to chase a lure in a long straight line, and then practice making high speed turns by chasing a lure in a small circle. The next step is introduction to the schooling track, where the trainees get their first look at a real track lure and will eventually learn to break from a starting box and run with other dogs.

Win, Place, Show . . . or Go

Yet another change of home may occur when the greyhound goes to the racing kennel, which usually houses about 60 dogs. A dog will spend the season at the same track, but may change tracks the next season. Each greyhound may race every three to seven days. Dogs start at the bottom, proving themselves against other novice greyhounds. When they win a

Greyhound adoption has found loving homes for many ex-racers, such as this retiree lounging in an X-pen during an adoption promotion.

race, they move up to compete in a tougher class. Only a few will ever get to race in Class A; only the best will ever win in it. After a number of losses (depending on class), they move down to a lower class. When they eventually can't even win in Class D, or when they have an injury that will render

The dogs run for the joy of it, but their fate depends upon coming in first.

Track Facts

- Record U.S. race times are 29.51 seconds for 5/16 mile, 36.43 seconds for 3/8 mile, and 42.57 seconds for 7/16 mile. Although this works out to about 37 miles per hour (59.5441 km/hr), the greyhound's top speed on the straightaway is closer to 45 miles per hour (72.4185 km/hr).
- Greyhound racing is the sixth largest spectator sport in the United States.
- The all-time top earner is Mo Kick, who won over $300,000 from 1991–1994.
- There are about 50 tracks in 16 states.
- Eight greyhounds usually run in a race.
- Dogs wear muzzles for protection and to determine the winner in a photo finish.
- Greyhounds begin racing at about 17 months of age and must retire by age six years.
- Every dog is tattooed with an identification number in each ear at the age of three months. Right ear number indicates the month and year of birth, and a letter indicating the sequence of the individual dog within a litter; left ear indicates the dog's NGA litter registration number.
- Only racing kennels with a contract at the particular track can enter races.
- Dogs are placed in a lockup area two hours prior to posttime.
- Greyhounds that weigh over 1.5 pounds (.66 kg) heavier or lighter than their recorded racing weight are not allowed to race.
- Urine samples are collected from winners to check for illegal drugs.
- The Greyhound Hall of Fame spotlights great racing dogs and is open to the public in Abilene, Kansas.

them noncompetitive, their race days are numbered.

Those dogs that have had illustrious careers may still have a future as a breeding animal. But most do not. This is where greyhound adoption comes in to play.

Fate of the Retired Racer

The American Greyhound Council was formed in the 1980s in part to advance the welfare of racing greyhounds. By promoting the adoption of retirees, underwriting many of the expenses, and encouraging a reduction in breeding, a milestone was reached in 1994: For the first time, more greyhounds were adopted (about 14,000) than were euthanized (about 13,000). Unless a dog is severely injured or has a personality problem, at most tracks every retiree has a chance at adoption.

There is a feeling among some of the public that racing greyhound owners and trainers are satanic beings who regularly abuse the dogs in their care. This perception is fueled by the well-publicized cases of greyhound kennels full of neglected dogs. The NGA has now implemented a tough surprise inspection program; those failing to make the grade are permanently banned from racing.

The truth is that greyhound people are no different from the rest of humankind. Both top-notch and unscrupulous pet owners as well as greyhound owners exist. The irresponsible greyhound owners have the chance to maltreat a lot of dogs at once. The expense involved in raising greyhounds makes their neglect a very stupid business practice, but sometimes people do very stupid things. Often people own so many greyhounds that they are financially on the edge, and when money fails to come in, the kennel is in dire straits. When money depends upon animals, animal welfare

They're off! With amazing acceleration, greyhounds reach maximum speed by their third stride out of the gate.

often sadly takes a back seat. As in all walks of life, there are those who take out their disappointments on defenseless animals. Some greyhounds are both neglected and abused.

Two major problems are at the root of the dog crisis in the United States—overbreeding and the inability to take lifelong responsibility for a dog. Racing greyhound breeders are guilty of both. Yet even they have lamented the fact that success in greyhound racing depends largely upon breeding so many dogs that a few are bound to

Photo finish! The tip of the muzzle determines the winner.

Many dogs that were not first over the finish line have found a place as first in their family's hearts.

Most track greyhounds wear a lightweight kennel muzzle when they are together so that no inadvertent bites occur. These muzzles allow plenty of ventilation and the dogs can even drink water while wearing them.

turn out winners. Breeders realize that everyone involved would be better off if they could agree to breed fewer

dogs, and from 1992 to 1994 they reduced the number of greyhounds born in the United States from 49,000 to under 39,000.

Greyhound racing is not a lucrative enterprise. In order to make a living by racing dogs, a trainer must know when to cut losses and give up on a dog that cannot earn its keep, and to do this without letting sentiment cloud logic. The rest of the kennel's welfare depends on it. It is simply not possible to make pets of the many dogs in a greyhound kennel. Keeping a dog in a cage for most of the day is not a pre-ferred way for a pet to live. Having been raised in this manner, however, most of the greyhounds in a well-run greyhound kennel are nonetheless well-adjusted to their lifestyle. They wag their tails and greet visitors with the gusto of any dog, but seem con-tent to spend most of their day snooz-ing. But once given the chance to live the life of a pet, they never look back.

Greyhound Choices

The AKC versus the NGA Greyhound

Such a choice—do you want a svelte and loving AKC greyhound, or a svelte and loving NGA greyhound? If you want your dog principally as a pet, you will be equally happy with either.

Probably the main consideration between an NGA or AKC greyhound is whether or not you must have a puppy. Although you could conceivably contact a track breeder and buy a puppy from a litter, you would pay a lot more money than necessary to buy a pet quality dog. Most NGA greyhounds become available only through greyhound placement groups after the dogs have finished their racing careers. Some may be yearlings that were either injured or didn't make the grade, but most are between two and four years of age. With a life expectancy of 10 to 14 years, this still gives you plenty of time. Still, you will not have the opportunity to share its puppyhood and shape its personality in the way that you may have dreamed. Having been raised in a kennel, home life will be totally foreign to these dogs. They may or may not be trustworthy with other pets. They do adjust to home life with incredible speed, however. In fact, these dogs combine the best of puppies and adults, in that you still have all the enjoyment of showing them the world, yet they are a lot smarter than puppies!

Puppies, while cute, are hard work. They chew, they mess the floor, they cry, they mess the floor, they run away, they mess the floor—they are mobile wetting machines loose in your home.

If you work away from home it may be especially difficult to care for a young pup. But if you must have a pup, you will almost certainly be getting an AKC greyhound.

Although both strains are clearly greyhounds, AKC greyhounds tend to be taller but narrower, with deeper chests, longer necks and legs, more arched backs, more angulated rear

The AKC greyhound is the ultimate in elegance, with a lithe, streamlined outline.

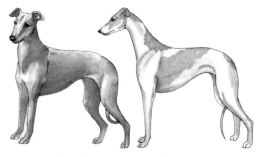

The NGA type greyhound as compared to the AKC type greyhound. The latter is taller and curvier, but narrower and with smaller bones and flatter muscles.

legs, longer, lower tails, and smaller, more tightly folded ears—in short, everything thought of as "greyhound" is essentially accentuated. They come in black, red, fawn, brindle, blue, or spotted, but the spotted and brindle are most common. If you want to try showing, you should get an AKC dog.

NGA greyhounds are longer and wider bodied, with thicker tails and bunchier muscles. Their fur may be less sleek, they have a greater tendency to have missing thigh hair, and the self-colors (no spots) predominate. Many have experience coursing after live quarry and will need to be introduced to other pets, such as cats, with extreme caution. NGA greyhounds have a tendency to be more keen for the chase, and are undeniably faster than AKC greyhounds. Because of this they also are more likely to run to the point of hurting themselves.

There are other considerations. If you live in an area where there is greyhound racing, it will be much easier to locate a local greyhound placement group. If you want an AKC greyhound, expect to have to look far afield no matter where you live, and to pay a little bit more for it.

Once you peer into the deep wells of the eyes of a greyhound awaiting adoption it's a good bet that you will not be able to leave without it, so make up your mind about your plans before going to visit. It is undeniably very special to save the life of one of these dogs and to know that you will give that dog the first real human companionship it has ever known. But the AKC greyhound puppy could need you just as much. Simply because it comes from show parents does not mean that it has a waiting home; many pet quality AKC pups are also in need of loving families but do not have the benefit of placement groups. In the end you must choose the dog that will bring mutual happiness.

Locating an NGA Greyhound

Greyhound adoption continues to grow in popularity, so the list at the end of this book is only a partial one. The NGA can also steer you to a source. Warning: Good greyhound placement agencies are very particular about where their "babies" are going. They will be happy to talk with you about the pros and cons of greyhound ownership, but don't expect to show up on a whim and leave with a dog.

Locating an AKC Greyhound

Most people who want an AKC greyhound want a show-quality dog. But even the finest show-bred litter often has one or more pet-quality puppies that would not make competitive show prospects. Such dogs are still beautiful animals but might have ears that don't fold properly or undescended testicles, for example. Keep in mind that most NGA dogs would be deemed pet quality rather than show quality. If you want a greyhound pet, and especially if you want to raise it from puppyhood, consider contacting a show breeder and asking for pet quality.

Note: You cannot get even a good pet quality greyhound from a pet store.

Show breeders can be located by contacting the Greyhound Club of

America or by perusing a dog magazine such as *Sighthound Review* or *Dog World*. The latter also has a schedule of dog shows, where you may be able to meet some greyhounds in the flesh. Be sure to arrive early; shows start at 8 or 9 A.M., and unless you know what time the greyhounds are being shown you risk missing them altogether.

However you contact breeders, let them know whether you are interested in show or pet quality, and exactly what your preferences are. Many hard feelings have resulted from misunderstandings about pet versus show quality. Don't ask for show quality if you have no intention of showing; it's not fair to the breeder who has bred with the intention of producing champions. And don't ask for pet quality if you have any intention of showing; it, too, is not fair to the breeder who would prefer that only the best stock represent their dogs in the show ring. And if you simply don't know, let the breeder know that, too, and perhaps some intermediate arrangement can be made.

Why You Can't Breed Your Greyhound

With the hordes of greyhounds clamoring to be adopted, it's not only difficult to justify breeding more, but also foolhardy to think that potential puppy owners would beat a path to your door.

Most ex-racers are neutered before being made available for adoption, nor will the NGA register puppies from adopted greyhounds (the owner would have kept the dog for breeding had it been breeding quality). And most AKC breeders will sell pets only with the agreement that they be neutered.

Caution: Unless you are an established breeder of show or coursing greyhounds, count on keeping every newborn puppy for the rest of its life. If you balk at keeping ten greyhounds for

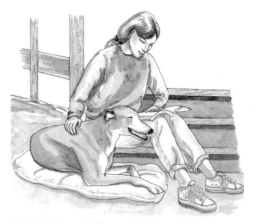

Both NGA and AKC greyhounds excel at relaxing, especially if it is next to their owner.

the next decade, you had best heed the following advice: Never, never, be tempted to breed a litter of greyhounds.

The Reality Check

Before going further, step back and consider fully what you are doing. A dog is not a trial-run item. It is a sentient being that will not understand why it is once again being uprooted from its home. Nor will it understand why it is being banished to the backyard. It will not understand that its family welcomed it into their home on a whim and then tired of it as they would another toy. When you invite a dog into your family, invite it as a real family member, not a passing fancy or a conversation piece. Many people argue that they are doing the ex-racer a favor by saving it from death and that it should be thankful for any home. There are fates worse than death for a dog, and a life of abuse, neglect, and isolation is one of them.

Count on having your greyhound for another ten years. Count on spending a lot of money on food and veterinary bills. Count on spending every day feeding, walking, and cleaning up after

Much like a thoroughbred foal, the gangly greyhound pup must grow into its legs.

hunting breeds in that they must act independently; a greyhound that paused to check back with its master while chasing a hare would be a very poor coursing dog. Greyhounds were bred to chase without question or human direction; they will be happy to chase cats and run amuck around the neighborhood, with or without your approval. Under no circumstances can your greyhound be trusted to stay in your yard without a leash or fence. A blowing bit of paper or squirrel seen across the street can spell disaster.

Most people are very surprised to discover how easy the greyhound is to live with. Another trait of the coursing dog as compared to other hunting dogs is that the coursing dog is bred for a quick burst of energy. Its job is over in minutes. Thus, like the cheetah, the greyhound tends to sleep for a large part of the day, conserving its energy for use in an explosive burst. Conversely, pointing, retrieving, herding, and sled breeds must be able to sustain high energy levels and remain alert for hours. They will maintain these levels inside of your home as well. Thus, if you want a quiet companion, consider the greyhound; but if you want a constant ball of fire, consider another breed.

Still, the greyhound needs the daily opportunity to burn that energy it has so carefully stored throughout the day. It's not fair to own a greyhound—especially a young greyhound—if you have no safe place to let it run.

Another important trait of hounds is that they have been selected to hunt and live together without fighting. A greyhound will occasionally get in an argument with another dog, but they will generally not look for trouble as the flight instinct is stronger than the fight instinct. Greyhounds live together well.

Greyhounds are extremely tolerant dogs, but they don't have the padding to protect them from rough children.

your dog. Count on making sacrifices, whether it be chewed shoes, soiled carpets, or compromised vacations. And count on your dog slowing down and not being quite so playful and entertaining as it grows older.

Don't get a dog just for the children. No matter how sincere a child's promises to take care of the dog might be, mom or dad often end up doing most of the work. It is not fair to the dog to use its missed dinner as a lesson to teach Junior the meaning of responsibility. Greyhounds are good with children, but not as playful as many children would like.

Don't give a dog as a gift or Christmas item. People should always make the decision about getting their own dog, and a dog deserves to be the center of attention when it arrives at its new home, not one of many trinkets amidst the hubbub of celebration.

The Greyhound as a Pet

Finally, think one last time whether the greyhound is the breed for you. Dog breeds differ as much in actions as in appearances. The greyhound is every bit as specialized in behavior as it is in form. Hounds differ from other

Greyhounds make good pets for gentle children, but don't go for rough and tumble play.

Dubbed the "40 mph couch potato," greyhounds make every attempt to live up to their "lazy old hound dog" heritage.

21

Their lack of eagerness for constant play may make them frustrating for some children. And beware that wagging whiplike greyhound tail: ouch!

Greyhounds are a "soft" breed and must be treated and trained gently. They learn quickly, but they become bored easily. They often respond to obedience commands with the speed of a tired slug. Greyhounds are used to doing as they're told, and are not a breed that will engage in dominance disputes. Although not as demonstrative as many breeds, the greyhound takes its commitment to family seriously and may not take easily to transferring homes once the attachment has been made.

Greyhounds are not eager barkers, and make poor watchdogs. They are not biters, and are worthless guard dogs.

Greyhounds can actually be good apartment dogs, as long as their owner is absolutely committed to a regular exercise regime for the dog. They sleep a lot and are accustomed to relieving themselves during scheduled outings, but again, they can never be let out unsupervised. Ex-racers are used to routine, and do not understand the concept of "in just a minute."

Many people compare the greyhound to a cat—independent, somewhat aloof, and very conscious of creature comforts. They love to be stroked and many will even rub against you in a catlike manner. Theirs is a quiet, dignified affection, more likely conveyed by resting their head in your lap than by licking or fawning. It is possible to train a grey-hound to stay off the furniture, but in all fairness you should supply a soft, preferably raised, bed of its own. The greyhound does not have built-in padding, and in fact it is prone to callus and bursa formation if deprived of soft bedding. Nor does it have built-in insulation, so it should be protected from extremes in temperature.

Greyhounds are by no means small dogs, with NGA males averaging from 65 to 85 pounds (29–39 kg), and NGA females from 50 to 65 pounds (23–29 kg). They will greet you by jumping up on you, and could inadvertently knock down a frail or unsuspecting person. Greyhounds can also scout your kitchen counters for tasty morsels and steal them with lightning speed. They do not believe in sleeping curled in a ball, but seem to prefer to stretch to their limits in order to take up as much room as possible (especially if sharing your bed). Food and boarding bills will be higher than those for a small dog. Greyhounds eat alot for their size.

The greyhound's coat is wash and wear. It has no undercoat and is not oily, which means that dirt does not cling to it. More important, no doggy odor!

The greyhound's quest for speed makes it more prone to injuries and lameness than other breeds. It is fearlessly drawn to moving cars as a nail is to a magnet.

Remember: A good fence, ready leash, soft bed, gentle touch, and warm heart are all necessities for greyhound ownership.

Welcoming Your Greyhound

Acquiring a greyhound is relatively easy—but welcoming a new family member will require planning. Let's face it: once that greyhound sashays through your front door, hops onto your couch, and turns those lustrous doeeyes upon you, your life may never be the same, so you might as well start preparing now. And because you'll want to spend your first days together getting acquainted, you need to have everything ready ahead of time.

Greyhound Essentials

A new greyhound could provide an excuse to go on a wild shopping spree. A visit to a large pet store or a dog show vendor aisle, or a glance through one of the pet supply mail-order catalogs will dazzle you with items you never even imagined a dog could use, much less need. But there are some essentials.

Collar: First, your greyhound will need a collar—two collars, in fact. A soft buckle collar is best for around the house, but a cloth choke collar is actually safer for walking in public, because the greyhound's comparatively thick neck and narrow head enables it to pull backward out of a buckle collar when startled. A problem with any collar is the tendency of the delicate hair on the underside of the neck to be worn off. Some owners fashion fabric "turtlenecks," either out of large socks with the foot cut out or a woman's tube top cut down the middle and sewn in half, to be worn around the neck and under the collar. Special collars with sheepskin lining can also be ordered or made. An identification tag should be affixed to the buckle collar.

Leash: A nylon, web, or leather leash is another necessity. Chain leashes are impossible to handle; just try restraining a lunging greyhound with a chain leash wrapped around or pulled through your fingertips. The retractable leashes are very handy, but be careful: when dropped, the handle retracts quickly toward the dog. Some dogs may think it is chasing them, causing them to run from it in fright—a very dangerous situation when dealing with a greyhound.

Bowls: You will need flat-bottomed food and water bowls. Stainless steel bowls are best; some dogs have an allergic reaction to plastic. Be sure to find out what your greyhound has been eating and try to feed the same food at first.

A buckle collar for around the house and a choke collar for walks are both needed for your greyhound's wardrobe.

The greyhound on its throne.

Toiletries and first aid: You will also need a soft brush and nail clippers, and should assemble your first-aid kit (see page 62). In most parts of the country you will need greyhound-safe flea control products (see page 47), and you need to schedule an appointment with your veterinarian so that you can start heartworm prevention.

Bed: Decide now whether you plan to share your bed with a bedhogging greyhound. Even kennel greyhounds that have never seen a bed seem to have a genetically programmed recognition of your bed as their resting throne. If you prefer private sleeping arrangements, provide your greyhound from the start with a bed of its own, either a spacious cage or a cozy cushion. Besides specially made dog beds, popular choices are a "Papa-san" chair cushion or a bean-bag chair, which works better if it is missing some of its beans.

Cage: Your greyhound will appreciate having a cage, especially at first, because a cage is its accustomed home. It is also an invaluable housebreaking aid, because your greyhound is accustomed to controlling elimination when in its "den" until time for a scheduled turnout. Greyhounds are also used to being fed in their cage, and may be confused initially if you feed them elsewhere. The cage can also keep your greyhound out of trouble when you can't always watch. Think of it as you would a baby's crib: a place for peace and protection. And just as with a child, the crib or cage is a place for bedtime and naptime, but not a place of exile or a place to spend entire days. As your greyhound's private quarters, the cage should be off limits to harassing children. Plastic cages are readily available, economical, and approved for airline shipping. Most greyhounds need the largest size. Wire cages allow more ventilation and visibility, and fold for easy storage and transport.

Pen: You may find an exercise pen (or "X-pen") to be a helpful purchase. These are transportable wire folding "playpens" for dogs, typically about 4 feet by 4 feet (1.3 m × 1.3 m). Buy the tallest size, usually 48 inches (1.3 m).

They make a handy indoor enclosure when you can't be watching, and are good for traveling. Baby gates are also a big help; dogs do not protest as much when blocked by a baby gate instead of a closed door, and the visibility allows you to supervise. Some of the anti-chew preparations (e.g. Bitter Apple) may help protect your furniture and walls, but do not rely exclusively upon these products. Adult greyhounds are luckily not big chewers, and would usually prefer a chew bone or a toy to furniture, once they know the difference.

Toys: Rawhide bones are excellent for satisfying the urge to chew, but small pieces can cause choking and rawhide cured overseas can contain toxic chemicals. Nylabones are a safe alternative. Some greyhounds enjoy balls and frisbees, others have no interest in them (try rolling, not throwing, them). All greyhounds enjoy a pole-lure (see page 75 under Greyhound Fitness). Greyhounds especially enjoy snuggling and playing with stuffed animals; just make sure the eyes and nose will not come off and avoid those stuffed with Styrofoam beads or straw unless you really enjoy vacuuming. Latex squeaky toys are also enjoyable (for dogs, but not always their owners!); make sure the squeaker is secure. The knotted cotton (never nylon) rope toys are popular and safe. Never give toys that are so small they could be inhaled and lodge in the windpipe. Homemade toys of plastic milk containers and stuffed socks are every bit as appreciated as their store-bought counterparts. But don't be tempted to use an old shoe; when your greyhound happens upon your closet full of new shoes it may think it has arrived at the toy store and start chewing!

Waste control: Shopping for a pooper-scooper may not sound like much fun, but in years to come this will be one of your best purchases. The two-piece rake type with long handles are best for the backyard. And you can get a doggy septic system that will devour all of the bounty. Don't lose your backyard because it resembles a minefield, and don't expect your greyhound to dance around trying to keep its feet clean. The right tools will help you get the scoop on poop.

Housing

In most climates, greyhounds cannot be kept as exclusively outdoor dogs. They have too little insulation to protect them from the cold or heat, and too little fur to protect them from summer insects. Despite the fact that an ex-racer may have grown up without a human family, it still lived with other greyhounds and so did have companionship. Such a dog becomes attached quickly to its new family and will not be happy separated from them for long periods.

It is best that the new dog not have the run of the entire house. Choose an easily greyhound-proofed room where you spend a lot of time, preferably one that is close to a door leading outside. Kitchens and dens are usually ideal. When you must leave your dog for some time, you may wish to place it in a cage, secure room, or outdoor kennel. Garages have the disadvantage of also housing many poisonous items; bathrooms have the disadvantage of being so confining and isolated that dogs may become destructive.

If you keep your greyhound outside while you are gone you must provide shelter, preferably a cozy doghouse. The ideal doghouse has a removable top for easy cleaning, and a windbreak so that the door does not lead directly into sleeping quarters. For your peace of mind, you may wish to place the house within a small absolutely secure kennel. Some people combine a kennel run with a doggy door leading to

The best food bowls are stainless steel, heavy enough so that they cannot be pushed around, and have a wide base to prevent tipping over.

an enclosure in a garage, or to a separate room in the house.

Important: Tying a greyhound, even on a runline, is a very bad idea. It renders the dog vulnerable to marauding dogs, whiplash, tangled legs, and even broken necks and choking. Don't do it.

Safeguarding Your Greyhound

If you've ever had to baby-proof your home, you have a head start on puppy-proofing. But the greyhound can reach a lot higher, run a lot faster, and chew a lot harder than any child. Put poisons out of reach—beware of rodent and snail baits, household cleaners, toilet fresheners, leaked antifreeze, drugs, some houseplants, even chocolate (especially baker's chocolate)—all can be deadly. Antifreeze is an especially insidious killer: it has a sweet taste that dogs adore, and a toxic effect that will kill unless treated immediately. Swallowed pennies and metal nuts and bolts can have tragic consequences; they stay in the stomach and gradually dissolve, releasing zinc, which destroys red blood cells. Even nonpoisonous items can be deadly when swallowed. Knives, needles, nails, bones, rocks, rings—all have been found in dogs' stomachs and all have proved fatal at times.

Young dogs love to chew the insulation from electrical cords, and even lick outlets. This can result in severe burns, loss of the jaw and tongue, and death. Running into a sharp table corner could cause an eye or shoulder injury. Cooking pots should never be where your greyhound could pull them down and be scalded. For its own safety, teach your greyhound that it is never allowed to jump up on kitchen counters. Do not allow a puppy near the edges of high decks, balconies, or staircases, and make sure that adults understand the heights involved. Greyhounds can slide on slick tile or wood floors. A rubber-backed carpet runner will help prevent falls. Wooden steps should be carpeted if possible.

Make it a household rule to close the toilet bowl lid. Any toilet bowl fresheners should be nontoxic to pets. Greyhounds see that magnificent porcelain bowl as the ultimate drinking fountain, but this is one of many instances when you know better.

A greyhound tail is long and fragile, and—far too often—missing, because it lags behind the rest of the dog and is easily caught in household and car doors, and even fans. Everyone in your family (and visitors too) must be made to understand the danger of slamming a door without first checking for tail clearance. Use doorstops to ensure that the wind does not suddenly blow doors shut. Be equally wary of the gap on the hinged side of the door, which can catch a wagging tail or even a foot.

Doors can pose other dangers. Be especially cautious with swinging doors; a dog may try to push one open, become caught, try to back out, and strangle. Sliding glass doors are difficult to see, and could severely injure a dog that tries to run though them. Place stickers at your dog's eye level on any glass door. And remember, a greyhound has no reason to suspect that ripping its way through a screen to save you the bother of opening the door won't be heartily appreciated by you. Consider adding heavy grills to screen doors. Finally, doors leading to unfenced outdoor areas should be kept securely shut.

Good fences make good neighbors—and old dogs. Your greyhound would probably love to go visiting all of your neighbors and help them exercise their cats. Loose greyhounds are a danger to themselves, other neighborhood free spirits, and drivers who might try to avoid hitting your car-senseless greyhound. Your dog should never, ever be allowed to roam the streets on its own. Not only is it dangerous for the dog; it will make both of you extremely unpopular. Few items can raise the ire of homeowners more than dog feces on their lawn, and with good reason. Other people should not be expected to take on your responsibility of cleaning up after your dog.

Greyhounds are capable jumpers, but they are not natural jumpers. They are careful dogs, and will seldom attempt something they are not sure they can do. This means that if your fence is good and tall (at least four feet [1.3 m]) in the first place, your greyhound will probably never jump it. But if your fence is weak and low, you will probably have an escape. And if you then try to add a little to the fence top, you will probably have another escape. In other words, you can inadvertently train your greyhound to jump Olympic height fences by raising your fence just a little at a time. Make sure your fence is unjumpable in the first place, and that the gate has a locking mechanism that not even Lassie could figure out. Invisible fences (which are actually underground wires that shock a dog wearing a special collar when it crosses over the wire) are not advisable, because not only can a fast greyhound get past the boundary before it

For its health as well as happiness, you must supply a soft bed for your greyhound.

realizes it, but they also allow stray dogs to get into what should be your greyhound's sanctuary. Wooden privacy, chain-link, or wire mesh fences are all good. Just make sure to eliminate with sharp edges or wires that can catch the skin.

Greyhounds can work up fairly good speed even in a small yard, so you must look for small stumps or pipes that could break or dislocate a toe, or bushes with sharp, broken branches at greyhound eye level. Check for poisonous plants. Some of the more deadly plants:
- yew
- mistletoe
- English holly berries
- philodendron
- Jerusalem cherry
- azaleas
- rhododendron
- foxglove
- water hemlock
- milkweed
- rattlebox
- corn cockle
- jimson weed
- jessamine
- oleander
- castor bean.

Note: If you have a pool, be aware that although dogs are natural swimmers, they cannot pull themselves up

Greyhounds love chasing stuffed bunnies (almost) as much as real ones.

a swimming pool wall and can drown if you have not provided a negotiable exit and taught your dog how to use it.

Safeguarding Your Home

Never leave your new greyhound in a room in which there is something you value that your pet can damage. Leather furniture is the world's biggest rawhide chewy, rivaled only in chewing appeal by wicker. Dogs particularly like to chew items that carry your scent. Eyeglasses, shoes, socks, and other clothing must be kept out of the greyhound's reach until it learns the ground rules. Remove books and papers. No need for a costly paper-shredder when you have a young greyhound! The greyhound's wagging tail can clear a coffee table and has a weedeater effect on fragile houseplants.

If you have carpeting, consider covering it with small washable rugs or a strip of indoor-outdoor carpeting until

your newcomer is housebroken. If you use an X-pen, cover the floor beneath it with thick plastic (an old shower curtain works well), and then add towels or washable rugs for traction and absorbency. Unless you have a puppy, the temporary housebreaking period should be very short and your house should be back to near normalcy within a couple of weeks.

The Homecoming

If possible, arrange to take a few days off from work so that you can spend time with your new family member. At the very least, bring your greyhound home on a weekend so that the first day in your home won't be spent alone. Even a former race dog will have minimal car experience, so it is best to bring a cage, a helper, or at least plenty of towels in case the dog gets car sick. Never let your new greyhound roam around the car, where it can cause and have accidents.

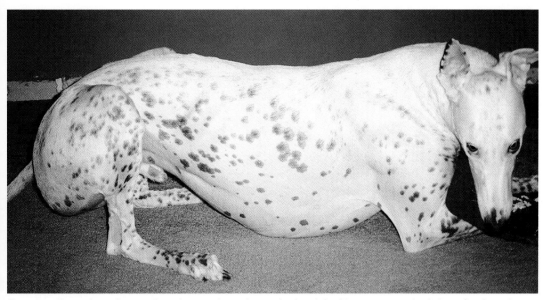

Even angelic greyhounds sometimes have a demonic streak when left with an unsupervised shoe. Greyhounds come in a rainbow of colors, but this white NGA dog with ticking is nonetheless unusual.

Arrange for the dog not to have eaten before leaving with you; this lessens the possibility of car sickness and helps it learn that you will be its new provider when you get to its new home. It's best not to stop to walk your greyhound unless you have a trip of over four hours.

Your greyhound should already know its name, but you can gradually introduce a new name by calling it both names at once, with the new name first. A greyhound of any age will learn a new name quickly, especially if it means food or fun is on the way. Make sure your chosen name does not sound like a reprimand or command; for example, "Nomad" sounds like "No."

When you get home, put the greyhound on lead and walk it to the spot you have decided will be the bathroom. Dogs tend to relieve themselves in areas where they can smell that they have eliminated before, so it is helpful to get that area established as

soon as possible. This is also why it is so critical to prevent accidents indoors, and to block access to areas in which dogs have had accidents. Once the dog has had a chance to relieve itself, let it explore a little and then offer it a small meal. Now is not the time for all the neighbors to come visiting. You want your dog to know who its new family members will be, and more people will only add to its confusion. Introductions to other family pets might also be better postponed.

Once the dog has eaten, take it back out to the part of the yard you have designated as the bathroom. Remember to praise enthusiastically when your greyhound eliminates in the right place. Once this has been accomplished, introduce your greyhound to its new accommodations and let it explore some more. When it begins to act sleepy, place it in its cage or on its sleeping pad so that it knows this is its special bed. A stuffed toy or rawhide

The cage should be a comfortable haven, with plenty of padding and a water pail clipped to the side.

chewy may help alleviate some of the anxiety of being left alone. You should place the cage or pad in your bedroom for this first night so that your new dog may be comforted by your presence. Remember, this is probably the scariest thing that has ever happened to your greyhound and the first time it has ever spent the night without other grey-hounds. It has no way of knowing that you are offering it a better life, and can only fear the unknown and miss its old friends. Make every effort to be comforting and reassuring on this crucial first night.

Your greyhound will probably be uneasy for some time after you turn its world upside down by bringing it into your family. You'll know that it has made the transition and formally adopted you the first time you catch it doing something utterly silly and so very unlike the public greyhound persona.

Life With a Greyhound

Just Say "No"

Decide before your greyhound comes home what parts of your home will be off limits. Your greyhound will be doing its best to understand the rules of this strange new world, and when you (or a kindhearted family member) let it break the rules "just this one time," you are not doing it any favor at all. Your dog will naturally want to explore its new surroundings and will think nothing of stepping onto the furniture for a better vantage point. A stern "No!" and firm but gentle push away from the furniture should let it realize that this is neither acceptable nor rewarding behavior. If your new greyhound wants to sleep on forbidden furniture, guide it instead to its own bed, and praise it when it stays put. The use of mousetraps on furniture, as advocated by some, is a great way to get to meet your new veterinarian quickly, and to learn all about damaged toes. There are several more humane items (available through pet catalogs) that emit a loud tone (or even a mild shock) when a dog jumps on furniture, but these should not be necessary if you train your greyhound consistently from the beginning.

You may have to teach your greyhound to go up and down steps. Most can go up easily, but should be encouraged to go slowly. Down is scarier; start near the bottom or with a short flight.

Housebreaking

If you cannot be with your greyhound for an extended period, you may wish to leave it outside (weather permitting) so that it will not be forced to have an indoor accident. One of the most important keys to successful housebreaking is never letting the first accident occur. But it will. Once it has, deodorize the area thoroughly, using a cleaner without ammonia, and if possible, place the area off limits temporarily. Your dog will need to urinate immediately after awakening, and soon after heavy drinking or playing. You will probably have to carry a young puppy outside to get it to the bathroom on time. Right after eating, or if nervous, your dog may have to defecate. Circling, whining, sniffing, and generally acting worried usually signals that defecation is imminent. Even if your greyhound starts to relieve itself, quickly but calmly pick it up (if a pup) and carry it outside. The surprise of being picked up will usually cause the puppy to stop in midstream, so to speak. You can add a firm "No," but yelling and swatting are neither necessary nor effective. The adult dog may be more difficult to hustle outside, but it, too, will get the message if you do your best to get it outside immediately, even if it means causing a trail to the door (this is where the throw rug or plastic sheeting comes in handy!). When your greyhound does relieve itself in its outside bathroom, remember to heap on the praise and let it know how pleased you are.

Because most track greyhounds have been trained to sleep in a cage with only a few scheduled bathroom breaks, they are especially easy to housebreak. Gradually enlarge the concept of the clean den by going from cage to X-pen to one room, with many "turnouts." At first, leave the cage, with its door open, in the room.

Greyhounds and Other Pets

Greyhounds are by nature amiable and not inclined to fight with other dogs. Greyhounds form close attachments to their housemates and will play and run together until exhausted when given a chance. Ex-racers are used to the constant presence of other dogs and may be very lonely at first. Consider adding another pet if you are gone for most of the day. In fact, while in many ways two dogs are better than one, three dogs can be better than two! With two dogs a problem can arise when one is left alone while you train or give personal attention to the other. With three there is always a pair left. Are four dogs better than three? No. Four dogs make one dog too many to catch and hold on to while walking off lead.

When introducing new dogs to each other, it is best if both are taken to a neutral site so that territoriality does not evoke protectiveness. Two people each walking a dog beside each other as they would on a regular walk is an ideal way for dogs to accept each other.

Greyhounds can get along with cats, but they need to be introduced cautiously. Some ex-racers may have live coursing experience, and although they can discriminate cats from rabbits, you need to give them a chance to see up close that there is a difference. From behind, a running cat looks a lot like a lure. Avoid letting the cat run from the dog; this would evoke a chase response. Dog-cat introductions are best made indoors, initially with a leash and muzzle. Let the dog see you hold, pet, and feed the cat, and then pet and feed the dog a wonderful treat. If the dog is fed every time the cat appears, it will come to really appreciate the cat. Until you are absolutely sure of your greyhound's behavior, do not leave the two loose home alone or outdoors. Many greyhounds have become fast friends with "their" pet cats.

Ex-racers can have a difficult time negotiating steps, and should be taught to do so slowly while on leash.

Forcing the dog to soil an area by not letting it out often enough will undo any housebreaking you may have accomplished. As a rule, dogs that continually soil their cage either have a cage that is too large, enabling them to walk to the other end to eliminate, or more commonly, this indicates a dog that is suffering from separation anxiety or a fear of being in the cage. An overly large cage can be divided with a secure barrier.

Greyhounds not only tolerate, but relish, the company of other greyhounds. This three-some each awaits its treat politely.

Note: Don't rely on keeping your dog and cat separated. No matter how careful, one day a mistake will be made, and it will not be your grey-hound's fault.

Weather Extremes

Greyhounds can thrive in almost any climate, but certain precautions must be taken in hot or cold weather. The greyhound coat is not a thick one, and in cold climates you will want a stylish coat or cozy sweater for your dog. Coats that fit greyhounds can be ordered from the NGA. Freezing weather brings other hazards. Dogs do not understand that the ice on frozen lakes can break, so you must be vigilant when around thin ice. As your greyhound romps in the snow, you must check its feet regularly for pads cut by ice or balls of frozen snow between the toes; these can be avoided by coating the dog's feet with oil. Walking on streets treated with salt will also be irritating to the paw pads, so be sure to rinse them upon return-ing home.

Summer can be even more danger-ous. Many dogs have died because their owners wanted to have them along on a trip to town and then left them in the car for "just a second." But when they got into the store there was a long line, and in the air-conditioned comfort of the store they lost contact with how hot it was outside—not to mention inside a closed car. Heatstroke also occurs as a result of another well-intentioned owner mistake: taking the dog for a romp in the summer sun. Dogs do not have sweat glands and must cool themselves through evapora-tion from the tongue. This system is not as effective as the human system, and dogs can become overcome by heat when their owners are scarcely affected. Unless you are taking your dog for a swim, in hot weather leave it at home in the daytime and schedule

HOW-TO:
Understanding Your Greyhound

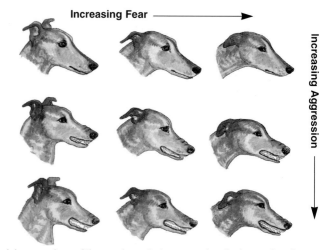

Increasing Aggression

Facial expressions of the greyhound, demonstrating the interactions between fearfulness and aggression.

In order to share your life with your greyhound, you need to realize that it inhabits a very different world from yours.

Vision: It is often claimed that greyhounds, as sighthounds, have vision superior to that of other dogs, but there is as yet no scientific evidence of this. No dogs see the world with as much detail or color as do humans. The dog's sense of color is like that of a "color-blind" person. That is, they confuse similar shades of yellow-green, yellow, orange, and red, but can readily see and discriminate blue, indigo, and violet from all other colors and each other.

The dog's eye is superior when it comes to seeing in very dim light. The eyeshine you may sometimes see from your dog's eyes at night is from a structure that serves to increase its ability to see in the dark.

Olfaction: The dog's sense of smell is renowned, and even the greyhound, eminently a sighthound, has olfactory abilities that are beyond our comprehension. It is as though we are completely blind when it comes to the world of smell, and there is no way we can imagine the vastness of this sensory world that is so very apparent to our dogs.

Taste: Dogs also have a well developed sense of taste, and have most of the same taste receptors that we do. Research has shown that they prefer meat (not exactly earthshaking news), and while there are many individual differences, the average dog prefers beef, pork, lamb, chicken, and horsemeat, in that order.

Dogs have sweet receptors similar to ours, which explains why many have a sweet tooth. But dogs' reception of artificial sweeteners is not like ours; these seem to taste bitter to them.

Hearing: Dogs can hear much higher tones than can humans, and so can be irritated by high hums from your TV or from those ultrasonic flea collars. The greyhound's folded ears are unencumbered by heavy fur and are ideally suited for detecting and localizing sounds, more so than the pendulous ears of other dogs.

Pain: Many people erroneously believe that animals cannot feel pain, but common sense and scientific research indicate that dogs and other animals have a well-developed sense of pain. Many dogs are amazingly stoic, however, and their ability to cope with pain is not totally understood at present. Because a dog may not express that it is in pain, you must be alert to changes in your dog's demeanor. A stiff gait, low head carriage, reluctance to get up, irritability, dilated pupils, whining, or limping are all indications that your dog is in pain.

Living with a dog gives you the opportunity to be a naturalist in your own living room, because dogs exhibit many of the same behaviors as their wolf ancestors. It has been theorized, however, that dogs differ from wolves in being perpetual juveniles; they never mature mentally to the same level that wolves do. This is one of the results of domestication, and breeds differ in the extent of this selected infantilism. Greyhounds hunt in a more wolflike fashion, so that in this

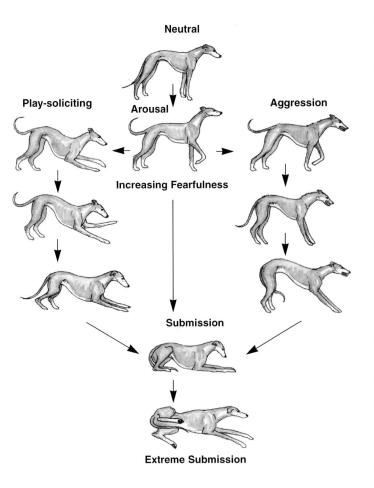

Neutral

Play-soliciting   **Arousal**   **Aggression**

Increasing Fearfulness

Submission

Extreme Submission

Greyhound body language.

sense they are less juvenile than most other breeds.

With careful observation, you can still see the wolf in your dog. Wolves and dogs depend upon facial expressions and body language in social interactions.

• A yawn is often a sign of nervousness. Drooling and panting can indicate extreme nervousness.

• A wagging tail, lowered head, and exposed teeth upon greeting is a sign of submission.

• The combination of a lowered body, wagging tucked tail, lowered ears, urination, and perhaps even rolling over is a sign of extreme submission.

• Raised hackles indicate wariness, or perhaps simply a chill due to cold weather.

• The combination of exposed teeth, a high, rigidly held tail, raised hackles, very upright posture, stiff-legged gait, direct stare, forward pricked ears, and perhaps lifting its leg to mark a tree indicates very dominant, threatening behavior.

• The combination of a wagging tail, front legs and elbows on the ground and rear in the air, with or without vocalizations is the classic "play-bow" position, and is an invitation for a game. Time for a romp!

With a longing look at the soft sofa cushion, a greyhound bows to the rule of the boss cat. Not domineering by nature, not only can greyhounds learn to live with cats, but may also allow themselves to be ruled by them!

Although sighthounds by definition, greyhounds have acutely developed senses of smell, taste, hearing, and touch.

your outings for early morning or evening. A wet terry cloth "cooling" jacket is a good idea even then. Even if all your dog does is loll in the yard all day, you must provide shade and plenty of cool water to prevent heatstroke. Some greyhound owners set up a fan in a safe location, and many provide a child's wading pool filled with water.

Greyhounds do not tolerate heat as well as other dogs of their build and coat type, and their owners must be especially careful not to let them overexert themselves in hot weather.

With summer also come insect bites and stings. Watch the edges of the ears for fly bites, and use an insect repellent if your dog must stay outside for long periods. Use any chemical repellent sparingly, and avoid those containing deet (diethyl-m-toluamide). If your dog is stung, remove the stinger and watch to make sure there is no allergic reac-

tion. A poultice of baking soda and water, followed by an ice pack, will help ease the pain, and a Benadryl (diphenhydramine) tablet can help thwart an allergic reaction or itching. A dog over 50 pounds (22.7 kg) can be given up to 25 mg (one capsule), once a day.

Summer brings another potentially dangerous event: the 4th of July. Every year dogs flee in terror from noisy fireworks. Secure your dog indoors on this festive occasion, and also during thunderstorms.

The Greyhound Abroad

Vacationing with your greyhound can be a disaster. Without proper planning, you will have to drive by most of the attractions you had meant to see, keep on driving when you are dead tired because all the motels turn you away, eat all of your meals at drive-ins, and admire the beaches from afar, all

37

because dogs are not allowed and it's generally not safe to leave one in the car.

But with proper planning, a vacation with your greyhound can be fabulous. Some attractions, motels, and beaches welcome dogs, if you know where to find them. Consult one of the several pet travel books available (such as *Gaines Touring With Towser* listed in the Useful Addresses and Literature section).

You should always travel with a cage. In the car it functions as a seat belt, and can also enable you to leave car windows down when you must leave the car for a minute (padlock the cage door for security). Motel owners and friends who have invited you to stay at their homes breathe sighs of relief when they see the cage coming inside. Your greyhound, too, will welcome the familiar refuge, especially if you must leave your dog alone for awhile. Never leave an uncaged dog in a strange place; it is too likely to feel you forgot it and might attempt to escape.

Wherever you go, try to make up for the bad behavior of those dog owners who think their little angel is above the rules, and who are ruining it for everyone. Always clean up after your dog. You can use a little plastic bag placed over your hand to pick up poop; turn the bag inside out and dispose of it in the closest trash can. Unsavory, perhaps, but not as bad as leaving it for someone to step in. Greyhounds are noticeable dogs. Wherever you go, you will be watched and will represent greyhounds to the public. Please be a good greyhound ambassador.

Air Travel: Shipping a dog by air should never be undertaken casually. Despite the fact that dogs ride in a special pressurized climate-controlled compartment, fatalities do occur, usually as a result of overheating during loading and unloading.

If you do ship your greyhound, arrange for the most direct flight in the coolest time of the day (preferably night), but avoid weekends. Most dogs are better off not given sedatives. You must use an airline-approved shipping kennel, padded with absorbent material. Put an elastic bungee around the door for extra protection, plaster your name all over the cage, and freeze a pail of water the night before. Clip the pail to the inside of the cage door; as the ice melts your dog will have drinking water that otherwise would have spilled out during loading. It's best to fly in the same plane with your dog, but if you must ship it alone, try to ship counter to counter rather than cargo.

Boarding

Sometimes you have no choice but to leave your greyhound behind. Ask the local greyhound adoption center for recommendations. The ideal kennel will have climate-controlled accommodations, preferably indoor/outdoor runs, and be accredited by the American Boarding Kennel Association. Make an unannounced visit to the kennel and ask to see the facilities. While you can't expect spotlessness and a perfumed atmosphere, runs should be clean and the odor should not be overpowering. All dogs should have clean water and at least some dogs, including any greyhounds, should have bedding. Good kennels will require proof of immunizations and an incoming check for fleas. They will allow you to bring toys and bedding and will administer medication as instructed. Strange dogs should not be allowed to mingle, and the entire kennel area should be fenced.

Your dog may be more comfortable if a pet sitter comes to your home and feeds and exercises it regularly. This works best if you have a doggy door. There are professional pet sitters, who are preferable to the kid next door because they can recognize problems and know what to do if your dog gets sick. They also understand how vital it is that your dog not get loose. Be very cautious before entrusting your greyhound to a neighbor or family member not accustomed to greyhounds. And always leave your veterinarian's name and emergency phone numbers.

Greyhound at Large

If your greyhound escapes or gets lost, you must act quickly to ensure its safe return. If your dog has recently escaped, don't wait for it to return. Go immediately to the worst place you could imagine its going. If you live near a highway, go there, and search backward toward your home. Be certain, however, that your dog does not find you first and follow you to the highway! And if you are driving, be certain that you do not drive recklessly and endanger your dog's life should it return to you. Then make up fliers and go door to door; check with any workers or delivery persons in the area. Call the local animal control, police department, and veterinarians. Make up large posters with a picture of a greyhound. Take out an ad in the local paper. Mention a reward, but do not specify an amount. Also do not mention your dog's NGA tattoo number. You will use this to verify that callers have really found your dog and are not trying to pull one of the many sick "I've found your dog but need money for its vet bills" scams.

Note: Your dog should always be wearing identification. A license tag is

Lost dog posters should be large and clear enough to be read from a passing car.

something anyone can read. Tattoos are permanent but many people don't know whom to contact with tattoo information. Microchip identification is becoming more popular, and many shelters now have scanners to read these chips.

Losing a dog is a very painful experience without closure. Act fast, and don't give up.

All dressed up and someplace to go.

Combining a playbow with a smile, a greyhound makes an irresistible invitation to play to its housemate.

Greyhound Nutrition

"You are what you eat" is as true for dogs as it is for people. Because your greyhound can't go shopping for its dinner, "it will be what you feed it," so you have total responsibility for feeding your dog a high-quality balanced diet that will enable it to live a long and active life. Dog food claims can be conflicting and confusing, but there are guidelines for selecting a proper diet for your greyhound.

First, the AAFCO (Association of American Feed Control Officials) has recommended minimal nutrient levels for dogs based upon controlled feeding studies. Unless you are a nutritionist, the chances of your cooking up a homemade diet that meets these exacting standards are remote. So the first rule is to select a food that states on the label that it meets the requirements set by the AAFCO. You should also realize that when you add table scraps and other enticements, you are disrupting the balance of the diet.

Second, feed a high-quality food from a name-brand company. Dog owners tend to be one of three types when it comes to feeding their dogs: the first tries to save a buck by feeding

Despite appearances, greyhounds eat a lot. Some greyhounds, especially older ones, appreciate eating while lying down or having their bowl set on a small table so that they don't have to bend down so far to reach the food.

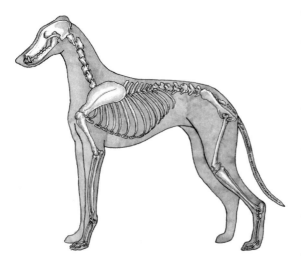

The skeletal system of the greyhound depends upon proper nutrition in order to develop normally. A greyhound in proper weight should have bones that are easily felt, but it should not look like a walking anatomy lesson.

dog food made from sawdust and corncobs, and then wonders why the dog has to eat so much of it; the other extreme chooses a food because it costs the most and is made from bee pollen, llama milk, and caviar yolks, (and of course, no preservatives) and then wonders why the food is rancid half the time and their dog is a blimp; and the third type buys a high-quality food from a recognized source that has proven their food through actual feeding trials. Avoid food that has been sitting on the shelf for long periods, or that has holes in the bag or grease that has seeped through the bag.

Finally, find a food that your greyhound enjoys. Mealtime is a highlight of a dog's day; although a dog will eventually eat even the most unsavory of dog foods if given no choice, it is unfair to deprive your family member of one of life's simple—and for a dog—most important, pleasures.

The Galloping Gourmet

Racing greyhounds eat a high protein diet typically consisting of about a pound (.5 kg) of raw "4D" meat (meaning from diseased, disabled, dying, and dead cattle) mixed with an equal amount of high-protein kibble, plus vegetables, milk, and other additives. Such diets are formulated to induce racing speed, but have not been tested for correlation to life expectancy. Racing greyhounds sometimes become quite sick from eating raw meat contaminated with salmonella, but trainers still believe that cooking the meat might do away with important components that influence performance. It would be more convenient for you and healthier for your greyhound if you switch to a good commercial food.

Many high-quality palatable commercial foods are available. Dry food is the most popular and economical, but most dogs, especially those used to eating meat and other goodies, find it the least palatable. It is also probably the healthiest, both in nutrient level and for dental hygiene. It is doubly important that dogs fed dry food have water available at all times. Canned foods are also popular as an additive to dry foods to increase palatability. The high moisture content of canned foods helps to make them tasty, but it also makes them comparatively expensive, because by weight you are in essence buying water. A steady diet of canned food would not provide the chewing necessary to maintain dental health. Semimoist foods are popular with some owners, but these, too, cannot provide proper chewing and also have the disadvantage of being fairly expensive and loaded with preservatives (mostly sugar-based). But many dogs enjoy them so they can be a reasonable choice for use in conjunction with a high-quality dry food. They are also very convenient when traveling.

Dog biscuits provide excellent chewing action, and some of the better varieties provide complete nutrition, but they can be expensive. Most people use them for snacks.

When comparing food labels, keep in mind that differences in moisture content make it very difficult to make comparisons between the guaranteed analyses in different forms of food. The components that vary most from one brand of food to another are protein and fat percentages.

Protein: Many high-quality foods boast of being high in protein, and with good reason. Protein provides the necessary building blocks for growth and maintenance of bones, muscle, and coat, and in the production of infection-fighting antibodies. Meat-derived protein is more highly digestible than plant-derived protein. Puppies and adolescent dogs need particularly high protein levels in their diets, which is one reason they are best fed a food formulated for their life stage. Older dogs, especially those with kidney problems, should be fed lower levels of very high-quality protein. Studies have shown that high-protein diets do not cause kidney failure in older dogs; but given a dog in which kidney failure exists, a high-protein diet will do a lot of harm.

Fat: Fat is the most calorie-rich component of foods, and most dogs prefer the taste of foods with higher fat content. Fat is necessary to good health, aiding in the transport of important vitamins and providing energy. Dogs deficient in fat often have sparse, dry coats. A higher fat content is usually found in puppy foods; obese dogs or dogs with heart problems should be fed a lower-fat food. Track greyhounds typically eat meat having a 15 percent fat content when young, and switch to a 7 percent fat content when racing.

Many greyhounds seem to be very sensitive to the amount of fat in their diet, with either too little or too much

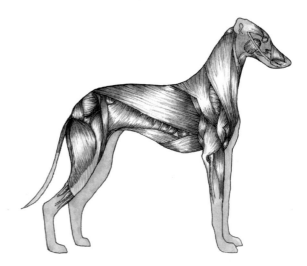

The musculature of the greyhound. Greyhounds have well developed muscles that depend upon protein for fuel.

resulting in diarrhea. A food with a fat content of around 15 percent produces good results in most greyhounds.

Choose a food that has a protein and fat content best suited for your dog's life stage, adjusting for any weight or health problems. There are a number of special diets available from your veterinarian that are especially designed for specific health problems. Also examine the list of ingredients: a good rule of thumb is that three or four of the first six ingredients should be animal-derived. These tend to be more palatable and more highly digestible than plant-based ingredients; more highly digestible foods mean less stool volume and fewer gas problems.

You may have to do a little experimenting to find just the right food, but a word of warning: One of the great mysteries of life is why a species, such as the dog, that is renowned for its iron stomach and preference to eat out of garbage cans, can at the same time develop violently upset stomachs simply from changing from one high-quality dog food to another. But it happens. So when changing foods you should do so gradually, mixing in progressively more and more of the new food each day for several days. Also, dogs will often seem to prefer a new food when first offered, but this may simply be due to its novelty. Only after you buy a six-month supply of this alleged canine ambrosia will you discover it was just a passing fancy.

Finally, let your greyhound help you choose. Find a food that your dog likes, one that creates a small volume of firm stool and results in good weight with a shiny coat. Be aware of the signs of possible food allergies (loss of hair, scratching, inflamed ears).

Keeping Your Greyhound Trim

The greyhound is naturally lithe and trim, but most people are so used to seeing dogs with a layer of blubber that they can't stand to see a greyhound in proper weight. As an athlete, your greyhound should have visible defined musculature, and the visible hint of the last three ribs. There should be a good tuck-up to the abdomen, no roll of fat over the withers, and no dimple at the base of the tail. The greyhound should have an hourglass figure, whether viewed from the side or from above.

Very young puppies should be fed three or four times a day, on a regular schedule. Feed them as much as they care to eat in about fifteen minutes. From the age of three to six months, pups should be fed three times daily, and after that, twice daily. Adult dogs may be fed once a day, but it is actually preferable to feed smaller meals twice a day. An aged dog will especially benefit from several small meals rather than one large one. Some people let the dog decide when to eat by leaving dry food available at all times. If you choose to let the dog "self-feed," monitor its weight to be sure it is not overindulging.

As dogs age, their metabolism and activity levels slow, so they need to be fed fewer calories. The same is true for most neutered and spayed dogs.

If your greyhound is fat, do not allow it to continue overeating. Try a less fattening food or feed less of your current food; make sure family members aren't sneaking it tidbits. If your greyhound remains overweight, seek your veterinarian's opinion. Obese greyhounds miss a lot of fun in life and are prone to joint injuries and a shortened life span.

Finicky eaters are a less common challenge. Many picky eaters are created when their owners begin to spice up the food with especially tasty treats. These dogs then refuse to eat unless the preferred treat is offered, and finally learn that if they refuse to eat even that proffered treat, another even tastier enticement will be forthcoming. Such dogs can profit from your limiting their feeding time to 15 minutes; what's left gets picked up. Give your greyhound a good, tasty meal, but don't succumb to

A greyhound in perfect weight and condition shows the hint of the last three ribs and the definition of muscles seen in this ex-racer.

greyhound blackmail or you may be a slave to your dog's gastronomical whims for years to come.

A Note on Bloat

Bloat, or gastric dilatation/torsion, is a deadly condition most common in large deep-chested breeds (see HOW-TO: Dealing With Emergencies, page 62). Greyhounds get bloat. The stomach becomes engorged with food, fluid, and gas, and then may twist on itself so that nothing can escape. Various types of food have been suspected, including diets high in soy or calcium, but research has not supported these ideas. Current recommendations are to avoid exercise for an hour before and after feeding, to feed at least two small meals a day, and to discourage the dog from gulping food or water or swallowing air.

Greyhound Maintenance

Coat and Skin Care

Even with its wash-and-wear coat, your greyhound will need a short grooming session once or twice a week to keep its coat gleaming and healthy. Use a natural bristle brush to distribute the oils, a rubber bristle brush to remove dead hair, and a flea comb to remove fleas or fine debris. Greyhounds have thinner and more sensitive skin than most dogs, especially between the thighs, around the armpits, and abdomen, and it can be damaged by harsh grooming or equipment.

Greyhounds rarely need bathing. Too much bathing, especially in an older dog, can dry the skin and result in dandruff. Try wiping away surface dirt with a damp sponge when possible. When bathing is necessary, it is best accomplished in the tub with a spray attachment and a nonslip mat. Use warm water (never hot) that would be comfortable for you if it were your bath. Place cotton balls in the dog's ears, and wash its entire body before starting on its head. Then rinse the head with a sponge, followed by the rest of the body with the spray.

You will get better results with a shampoo made for dogs. Dog skin has a pH of 7.5, while human skin has a pH of 5.5; a shampoo formulated for the pH of human skin can lead to scaling and irritation. Most shampoos will kill fleas even if not especially formulated as a flea shampoo, but none has any residual killing action on fleas. A variety of therapeutic shampoos exist for use with skin problems: moisturizers for dry scaly skin, antimicrobials for damaged skin, oatmeal-based antipru-ritics for itchy skin, and antiseborrheics for dandruff (the human shampoo Selsun-Blue has a doglike pH and is effective on dandruff). Finally, no one should be without one of the shampoos that requires no water or rinsing. These are wonderful for puppies, emergencies, and spot-baths. Always rinse other shampoos thoroughly, as any residue can be irritating. When finished, dry the dog adequately and do not allow it to become chilled.

Skin and Coat Problems

Itchy skin most often results from flea infestation, sarcoptic mange, or allergies to food, airborne particles, grass, or flea saliva. First make sure that not a single flea is on your dog. If scratching continues, you and your veterinarian will have to play detectives. Mange mites can be detected through skin scrapings, but allergies are more difficult to diagnose. Chewing, licking, and scratching, especially of the feet, ears, and groin, or rubbing the face are common signs of allergy. Pollen, household dust and mold, new carpets, or even animal dander can trigger inhalant allergies. Desensitization treatments are available, but your veterinarian must first perform tests to pinpoint the culprit.

Food allergies can also cause itching, but they are not as common as inhalant allergies. Feeding a food your greyhound has never before eaten may help, but you must feed that food exclusively (no treats!) for several weeks before expecting to see results. Lamb and rice diets became popular for dogs with food allergies because most dogs

The flea, dogdom's number one public enemy.

have never eaten lamb and rice, but these ingredients are not intrinsically hypoallergenic. Corticosteroid therapy can bring some relief from the itching, no matter what the cause.

In some cases hair is lost without itching. Demodectic mange, thyroid deficiency, estrogen excess, ringworm, and seborrhea are all possibilities that your veterinarian can diagnose.

Bald thigh syndrome, wherein hair is lost from the rear and sides of the thighs, is commonly seen in racing greyhounds. It reportedly appears about a month after intensive training begins, and may have a hereditary component. One theory is that it is due to either low thyroid or high corticosteroid production, in turn related to the stress of training. Treatment may include thyroid supplementation and a reduction of stressful exercise. More often the condition does not respond to any therapy, because there are no remaining hair follicles, supporting an alternate theory that the condition is a form of pattern baldness of possible hereditary origin that would have occurred regardless of training.

Calluses on the chest and elbows can be from lying on hard surfaces, but even carpet fibers can cause hair loss. Blisters and brown crust on the stomach, especially of puppies, can indicate impetigo. Clean the area twice daily with dilute hydrogen peroxide or surgical soap, and treat with a topical antibiotic.

Making Fleas Flee

Fleas on a greyhound are easy to detect. Their favorite greyhound spots are around the neck, the inner thighs, the lower back, stomach, and loin. They leave behind a black pepperlike substance (actually flea feces) that turns red upon getting wet. Some greyhounds develop an allergic reaction to the saliva of the flea; one flea bite can

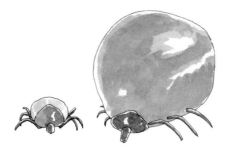

A tick before and after feeding.

cause them to itch and chew for days. Flea allergies are typically characterized by loss of coat and little red bumps around the lower back and tail base.

Flea control can be difficult, but it is not impossible. Any flea control program must be undertaken with care, because overzealous and uninformed efforts may lead to the death of pets as well as pests. Greyhounds are especially sensitive to flea products. Insecticides can be categorized as organics, natural pesticides, cholinesterase inhibitors, insect growth regulators, and systemics.

Collars: Never use a flea collar or medallion on a greyhound. They irritate the sensitive neck skin, cause nausea, and have a greater chance of killing your greyhound than they do a flea. The ultrasonic flea-repelling collars have been shown to be both ineffective on fleas and irritating to dogs.

Food additives: Scientific studies have also shown that feeding dogs brewer's yeast, as has been advocated for years by many dog owners, is ineffective against fleas.

Organics (e.g. D-Limonene) break down the outer shell of the flea and cause death from dehydration. They are safe, but slow-acting and have no residual action. Diatomaceous earth also acts on this same principle, but some researchers have expressed

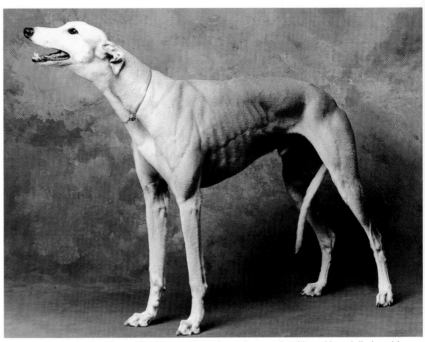

Your greyhound will look and feel better if you keep its coat healthy with a daily brushing.

concern that breathing its dust can be dangerous to dogs. Natural grade diatomaceous earth is probably safe; pool grade is not recommended because it is too finely ground.

Borax derivative formulations for the carpet are greyhound-safe and effective against fleas.

Natural pesticides (e.g. Pyrethrin, Permethrin) are relatively safe and kill fleas quickly, but have a very short residual action. They do not remain in the dog's system and so can be used frequently. They are greyhound-safe.

Cholinesterase inhibitors (Dursban, Diazinon, Malathion, Fenthion, Sevin, Carbaryl, Pro-Spot, Spotton) act on the nervous systems of fleas, dogs, and humans. They are used in yard sprays, dog sprays and dips, flea collars, and systemics. They kill effectively and have fairly good residual action, but must be

used with caution in any breed, and are not advisable for use on greyhounds. Some of these products specify that they are not approved for greyhound use.

The systemics are drugs that are applied to the dog's skin for absorption into the blood, or given orally, so that the flea dies when it sucks the blood. They must be avoided with greyhounds.

It is extremely important that you be aware of which chemicals are cholinesterase inhibitors. Ask your veterinarian when in doubt. Using a yard spray in conjunction with systemics, or some sprays and dips, or with certain worm medications that are also cholinesterase inhibitors can be an especially deadly combination.

Insect growth regulators (IGRs) prevent immature fleas from maturing and have proven to be the most highly effective method for long-term flea

An ex-racer and top coursing dog illustrates the typical pattern of bald thigh syndrome.

control. Precor is the most widely used for indoor applications, because it is quickly broken down by ultraviolet light. Fenoxicarb is better for outdoor use because it is resistant to ultraviolet light. IGRs are nontoxic to mammals but are expensive.

A new type of IGR on the market are the nematodes that eat flea larvae. Studies show them to be effective and safe. They must be reapplied regularly since they die when their food supply (the current crop of flea larvae) is gone.

Another recent development is lufenuron, a once-a-month pill that renders fleas that suck that dog's blood sterile. It is safe for greyhounds. All dogs and cats in the household must take the pill, and it may take several months before all fleas in the environment have reached sexual maturity and die out.

One final warning: There is a popular product on the market that contains "deet" (diethyl-m-toluamide: the same chemical found in some human insect repellents). It has been implicated in the death of many dogs, and is not recommended for greyhounds.

The flea comb is the safest flea control product: a comb with such finely spaced teeth that it catches fleas between them. Have a cup of alcohol or a running faucet handy for disposing of the fleas. A cotton ball soaked in alcohol and applied to a flea on the dog will also result in the flea's demise.

Because only about one to ten percent of your home's flea population is actually on your dog, you must concentrate on treating your home and yard. These are best treated with a combination greyhound-safe adult flea killer and

It is easier to cut the nails if the paw is held so that the pad is facing up.

IGR. Wash all pet bedding and vacuum other surfaces regularly, and especially before applying insecticides. Be sure that sprays reach into small crevices. Outside, cut grass short and spray in all areas except those that are never shaded (fleas do not mature in sunny areas). Repeat the entire procedure in two weeks.

It is not easy, but you can win the battle. A combination of pyrethrin spray and lufenuron for the dog, pyrethrin and IGR for the house and yard, or borax product for the carpets and nematodes for the yard, along with vacuuming and flea combing, should wipe fleas out. Every time you feel like giving up, consider how your greyhound deserves to live: free of the constant itching caused by a colony of bloodsucking parasites.

Ticks: Ticks can carry Rocky mountain spotted fever, Lyme disease, babesiasis, and most commonly, "tick fever" (erlichiosis), all potentially fatal diseases. Use a tissue or tweezers to remove ticks, as some diseases can be transmitted to humans. Grasp the tick as close to the skin as possible, and pull slowly and steadily, trying not to leave the head in the dog. Often a bump will remain after the tick is removed, even if you got the head. It will go away with time. Contact your veterinarian if your dog is listless or shows any signs of illness afterward.

Mange mites: Greyhounds are prone to two very different forms of mange. Sarcoptic mange is highly contagious, characterized by intense itching and often scaling of the ear tips, but is easily treated with insecticidal dips. Demodectic mange is not contagious and does not itch, but can be difficult to cure. It tends to run in families, and is characterized by a moth-eaten appearance, often on the face or feet; advanced cases lead to serious secondary infections. Some localized forms may go away on their own, but more widespread cases will need a special dip regime prescribed by your veterinarian. To effect a cure, you must strictly adhere to the dip schedule.

Nail Care

Professional greyhound trainers know that a dog is only as good as its feet, and the fastest way to ruin feet is to let them end in bear claws. When you can hear the pitter-patter of little feet, that means that with every step the nails are hitting the floor, and when this happens the bones of the foot are spread, causing discomfort and eventually splayed feet and lameness. If dewclaws are left untrimmed, they can get caught on things more easily or actually loop around and grow into the dog's leg. When the dog is standing, the nails should not touch the floor. You must prevent this by trimming your dog's nails every week or two.

Most ex-track dogs are very cooperative about having their nails cut, but for that occasional dog that thinks you are out for blood, you need to start at the beginning. Handle the feet and nails daily, and then clip only the tips of the nails, taking special care not to cut the quick (the central core of blood vessels and nerve endings). A guillotine-type nail clipper is easier to use with a large dog. Bribing with a tidbit after each toe works wonders. It's easier to cut the nails with the foot held behind the dog, so that you are looking at the bottom of the toes. You will see a solid core culminating in a hollowed nail. Cut the tip up to the core, but not beyond. On occasion you will slip up and cause the nail to bleed. Of course your greyhound will take this opportunity to let the neighbors know to call the authorities, but in truth it's not likely to be fatal. The bleeding is best stopped by styptic powder, but if this is not available, dip the nail in flour or hold it to a wet tea bag. Then hand your greyhound your sincere apology and a dog bone!

Ear Care

You should examine both inside and outside your greyhound's delicate ears during your grooming session. Fly bites can sometimes irritate the outer edges, and can be treated with a soothing cream. Trauma can result in broken blood vessels and an accumulation of blood (hematoma) in the ear tip, which must be treated promptly by your veterinarian. Greyhound ear tips are also susceptible to a condition called chilblains, in which the tips become itchy, dry, cracked, and even bloody in cold weather. The condition is due to poor blood circulation through the small capillaries of the ear tips. Mild cases can be treated with a topical antibiotic, and by keeping the ears warm and covered. Use a cut-off sweater sleeve or big sock with the foot cut out to hold the ears snug against the head. See your veterinarian if you don't see immediate improvement.

Dirt and wax in the ear can be removed by swabbing with mineral oil.

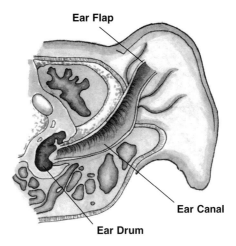

Ear Flap

Ear Canal

Ear Drum

The ear of a dog has both a vertical and horizontal canal. This provides an ideal place for fungal and bacterial infections, which can only be reached with liquid ear cleaners and medications.

Do not reach farther than you can see. Do not use alcohol, which can dry and irritate the ear, or ear powders, which can cake in the ear. Ear cleaners, available from your veterinarian, are the best solution for maintaining ear health. If the ear continues to have an excessive discharge, it may be due to a fungal or bacterial problem, which must be treated by your veterinarian. It could also be due to ear mites.

Ear mites: Tiny but irritating, ear mites are highly contagious and often found in puppies. An affected dog will shake its head, scratch its ears, and carry its head sideways. There is a dark waxy buildup in the ear canal, usually of both ears. If you place some of this wax on a piece of dark paper, and have very good eyes, you may be able to see the culprits, appearing as tiny white moving specks. Although there are over-the-counter ear mite preparations, they can cause worse irritation. Ear mites should be treated by your veterinarian.

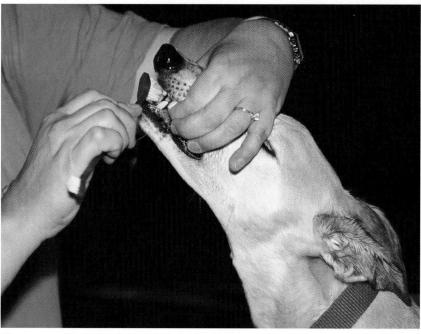

The time you take to brush your dog's teeth will pay off in lower vet bills and a healthier dog. The greyhound is an extremely cooperative dog and accepts this routine calmly.

Dental Care

Between four and seven months of age, greyhound puppies will begin to shed their baby teeth and show off new permanent teeth. Often baby teeth, especially the canines ("fangs"), are not shed, so that the permanent tooth grows in beside the baby tooth. If this condition persists for over a week, consult your veterinarian. Retained baby teeth can cause misalignment of adult teeth.

Check the way your greyhound's teeth meet; in a correct bite, the bot-

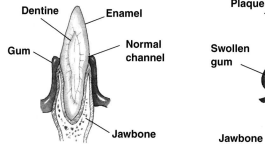
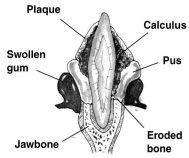

Normal tooth, left, and infected tooth, right.

The older greyhound appreciates a soft spot in the sun but still likes to be included in family outings.

tom incisors should touch the back of the top incisors when the mouth is closed. Deviations from this can cause chewing problems and discomfort. Extreme deviations may need to be examined by a veterinarian.

Greyhounds seem to have a particular problem with plaque and tartar accumulation, which worsens with increasing age. Dry food and hard dog biscuits can help, but cannot do the job alone. Rawhide chewies and large beef knuckle bones are better at removing plaque, but still not totally effective. The plaque can be removed by brushing the dog's teeth once or twice weekly with a child's toothbrush and doggy toothpaste. You can also rub the teeth with hydrogen peroxide or a baking soda solution on a gauze pad to help remove tartar. If not removed, plaque will attract bacteria

Health, nutrition, exercise, and happiness go hand in hand.

and minerals, which will harden into tartar. If you cannot brush, your veterinarian can supply cleansing solution that will help to kill plaque-forming bacteria, as well as bad breath. You may have to have your veterinarian clean your greyhound's teeth as often as once a year.

Neglected plaque and tartar can cause infections to form along the gum line. The infection can gradually work its way down the sides of the tooth until the entire root is undermined. The tissues and bone around the tooth erode, and the tooth finally falls out. Meanwhile, the bacteria may have been picked up by the bloodstream and carried throughout the body, causing infection in the kidneys and heart valves.

Greyhounds are especially prone to plaque accumulation and periodontal disease. There is no such thing as a doggy denture, so help your greyhound keep its teeth into old age by keeping its teeth sparkling throughout its life.

The Health Check

A weekly health check should be part of your grooming procedure. The health check should include the following examinations:
• eyes for discharge or cloudiness
• ears for bad smell, redness, or discharge
• mouth for red swollen gums, loose teeth, or bad breath
• skin for parasites, hair loss, or lumps.

Most bumps and lumps are not cause for concern, but because there is always a possibility of cancer, they should be examined by your veterinarian. This is especially true of a sore that does not heal, or any pigmented lump that begins to grow or bleed. Observe your dog for signs of lameness or incoordination, or for behavioral change. Run your hands over the muscles and bones and check that they are symmetrical from one side to the other. Check the toes, nails, and pads. Weigh your

dog and observe whether it is putting on fat or wasting away.

Doggy odor is not only offensive; it is unnatural. Greyhounds are not a stinky breed, and a dog that becomes odoriferous is likely a dog that has developed a problem. Don't exile the dog or hold your breath. If a bath doesn't produce results, it's time to smell your smelly dog. Use your nose to pinpoint the source of the problem. Infection is a common cause of bad odor; check the gums, the ears, the feet, the genitals, and the anus. Generalized bad odor can indicate a skin problem, such as seborrhea. Don't ignore bad odor, and don't make your dog take the blame for something you need to fix.

The Senior Greyhound

With good care and good luck your greyhound will grow old. Pat yourself on the back for a job well done, but be ready to be twice as diligent in caring for your dog now. When does old age start? It varies with breeds and individuals, with the average greyhound showing early signs of aging by seven years, and more advanced signs by nine years. You may first notice that your greyhound sleeps longer and more soundly than it did as a youngster. Upon awakening, it is slower to get going and may be stiff at first. It may be less eager to play and more content to lie in the sun. Some dogs become cranky and less patient, especially when dealing with puppies or boisterous children.

Ex-racers may have accumulated a number of injuries in their careers, and these injuries may come back to bother them in the form of arthritis. Aspirin, 5–10 mg/lb (10–25 mg/kg) body weight, twice daily, may help alleviate discomfort; be sure to use Ascriptin (or comparable brand), which is less likely to cause stomach bleeding. A "standard" aspirin is 325 mg.

Older dogs may seem to ignore their

owner's commands, but this may be the result of hearing loss. The slight haziness that appears in the older dog's pupils is normal and has minimal effect upon vision, but some dogs may develop cataracts. These can be removed by a veterinary ophthalmologist if they are severe.

Both physical activity and metabolic rates decrease in older animals, meaning that they require fewer calories to maintain the same weight. It is important to keep your older dog active, but calm exercise is preferable to full-blast running. Older dogs that continue to be fed the same as when they were young risk becoming obese; such dogs have a greater risk of cardiovascular and joint problems.

Older dogs should be fed several small meals instead of one large meal, and should be fed on time. There are a variety of reduced calorie, low protein senior diets on the market. But most older dogs do not require a special diet unless they have a particular medical need for it (e.g., obesity: low calorie; kidney failure: low protein; heart failure: low sodium). Dogs with these problems may require special prescription dog foods, available from your veterinarian.

Like people, dogs lose skin moisture as they age, and though dogs don't wrinkle, their skin can become dry and itchy. Regular brushing can stimulate oil production.

There is evidence that the immune system may be less effective in older dogs. This means that it is increasingly important to shield your dog from infectious disease, chilling, overheating, and any other stressful conditions. Older dogs present a somewhat greater anesthetic risk. Most of this increased risk can be negated, however, by first screening dogs with a complete medical workup, which may include blood tests, radiographs, or an electrocardiogram (ECG).

Long trips may be grueling, and boarding in a kennel may be extremely upsetting. Introduction of a puppy or new pet may be welcomed and encourage your older dog to play, but an especially boisterous pup will more likely be resented and be an additional source of stress.

The older dog should see its veterinarian at least semiannually, but the owner must take responsibility for observing any health changes. Here are some of the more common changes, along with some of the more common conditions they may indicate in older dogs:

• Limping: arthritis, ruptured cruciate ligament, toe problems, osteosarcoma
• Nasal discharge: tumor, periodontal disease
• Coughing: heart disease, lung cancer
• Difficulty eating: periodontal disease, oral tumors
• Decreased appetite: kidney, liver, or heart disease, pancreatitis, cancer
• Increased appetite: diabetes, Cushing's syndrome
• Weight loss: heart, liver or kidney disease, diabetes, cancer
• Abdominal distension: heart or kidney disease, bloat, Cushing's syndrome, tumor
• Increased urination: diabetes, kidney or liver disease, cystitis, Cushing's syndrome
• Diarrhea: kidney or liver disease, pancreatitis

This list is by no means inclusive of all symptoms or problems they may indicate. In general, any ailment that an older dog has is magnified in severity compared to the same symptoms in a younger dog. The owner of any older dog must be even more careful and attentive as the dog ages. A long life depends upon good genes, good care, and good luck.

An older dog may sleep longer and requires calm exercise rather than full-blast running.

In Sickness and in Health

Greyhound Physiology Is Different

Among the most specialized of breeds, the greyhound has correspondingly specialized physiology.

Not only is the greyhound big-hearted in terms of being sweet-natured, but also physically in relation to its body size. The greyhound heart is about the size of a human fist—approximately one third larger than the heart in comparably sized breeds. This is due to heredity, lean body mass, and the early heavy exercise regime that greyhounds undergo. The heart rate is also slower than in other dogs. Veterinarians not familiar with greyhounds may erroneously believe the large size and low rate to be indicative of disease.

Greyhounds also have higher blood pressure than other breeds. A systolic pressure of 180 would be considered hypertensive for most dogs, but is normal for a greyhound. The blood itself differs from that of other dogs, with a higher red blood cell count, lower white blood cell count, and lower platelet count. There are eight different blood types in dogs, but approximately 70 percent of greyhounds have the type that enables them to be universal blood donors—twice the percentage found in other breeds. This, combined with the other healthy attributes of the greyhound's blood, has made greyhounds valuable as occasional blood donors at veterinary hospitals.

Normal greyhounds often have blood tests that indicate abnormally low levels of thyroid hormones. In such dogs with "bald thigh syndrome" thyroid supplementation sometimes helps, but in most cases it does not. Some people believe that the low thyroid levels are typical for the breed, however, and supplementation for a dog that otherwise shows no deficiency is controversial.

Not surprisingly, the greyhound has a lower body fat percentage and higher muscle mass than most other breeds. This condition is not without its drawbacks. It means less energy reserve in times of illness. The low fat also means that the greyhound has very little insulation, resulting in the greyhound's tendency to overheat easily, as well as proneness to muscle cramping due to the buildup of lactic acid after hard exercise.

The low fat ratio has also been implicated in the greyhound's notorious anesthetic risk. Barbiturate-containing or sulfur-containing anesthetics such as Pentothal should never be used with greyhounds. Because these anesthetics are metabolized through fat, greyhounds have a hard time recovering from them. Anesthetizing dogs typically involves two steps: first administering an induction agent that renders the dog unconscious, and then administering an inhalant gas to maintain an anesthetized state. Isoflurane gas is a safe inhalant agent for greyhounds, but many veterinarians still use induction agents that are dangerous for a greyhound. Always insist that your veterinarian use a dissociative induction agent such as a ketamine/valium mixture or similar agent, or the human

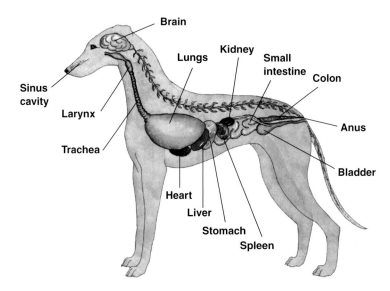

The internal organs of the greyhound.

drug propofol. Greyhounds are also very sensitive to acepromazine, a drug often prescribed to calm dogs. If used at all, it should be used at a far lower (at least one half) dosage than normally prescribed.

Greyhounds seem prone to skin lacerations, due in part to their thin coats and high speed. Most need suturing at some time in their life. In addition, like all breeds, the greyhound carries its own genetic baggage of hereditary disorders:
• Hemophilia A, factor VIII or AHF deficiency (blood clotting disorder resulting in prolonged bleeding).
• Esophageal achalasia (opening from esophagus to stomach does not allow proper swallowing, resulting in vomiting of undigested food).
• Azoturia (excessive nitrogen compounds in urine, resulting in severe cramping and stiffness after strenuous exercise).
• Gastric dilatation/torsion (bloat: emergency condition in which the

stomach enlarges and then twists, cutting off blood supply to some organs and resulting in shock and death within hours).
• Predisposition to dystocia (whelping difficulties).
• Short spine (malformed vertebrae).
• Lens luxation (displacement of the lens in the eye).
• Calcium gout (calcinosum circumscripta: painless nodules under skin on limbs).
• Predisposition to osteosarcoma (bone cancer).
• Predisposition to malignant hyperthermia (a problem that causes body temperature to soar when the dog is anesthetized, resulting in death).

None of these disorders is rampant in the breed, however. Hip dysplasia, so common in other large breeds, is almost unheard of in the greyhound.

Ex-racing dogs may come with a variety of common racing injuries, including healed fractures and torn ligaments, tendons, and muscles. Some may develop arthritis because of these old injuries.

Choosing Your Veterinarian

Because greyhound physiology is different, and because many veterinarians have little exposure to greyhounds, it is important to choose your veterinarian carefully. If possible, find one familiar with greyhounds, or at least one who is willing to listen to you concerning greyhound specifics. Availability, emergency arrangements, costs, facilities, and ability to communicate are also important. Your veterinarian should listen to your observations and should explain to you exactly what is happening with your dog. When you take your greyhound to the veterinary clinic, hold your dog on leash; if you think your dog may have a contagious illness, inform the clinic beforehand so that you can use another entrance.

Greyhounds are extremely cooperative patients, and many procedures that would require sedation with other breeds can be performed with the aid of a firm hold and a soothing voice. Discuss this option with your veterinarian and you may both be pleasantly surprised.

Medications

Giving medications to your greyhound is easy. Place pills as far back in the mouth as possible, close the mouth, and gently stroke the throat until your dog swallows. Wetting capsules or covering them with cream cheese or some other food helps prevent them from sticking to the tongue or roof of the mouth. For liquids, tilt the head back and place the liquid in the pouch of the cheek or rear of the tongue. Then close your dog's mouth until it swallows. Always give the full course of medications prescribed by your veterinarian.

To take your dog's temperature, lubricate a rectal (preferably digital)

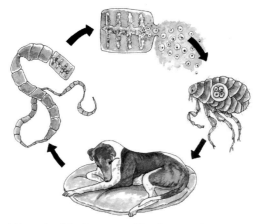

Life cycle of the tapeworm. Flea larvae eat tapeworm eggs shed in the dog's feces. When the dog later chews itself and ingests an adult tapeworm infected flea, the tapeworm is released to mature in the dog's intestinal tract.

thermometer and insert it about two inches. Do not allow your dog to sit down or the thermometer could break. Normal temperature is around 102°F (38.9°C).

Preventive Medicine

The best preventive medicine is that which safeguards against accidents: a well-trained dog in a well-fenced yard or on a leash, and a properly greyhound-proofed home. Other steps must be taken to avoid diseases and parasites, however.

Vaccinations

Rabies, distemper, leptospirosis, canine hepatitis, parvovirus, and corona virus are highly contagious and deadly diseases that have broken many a loving owner's heart in the past. Now that vaccinations are available for these diseases, one would think they would no longer be a threat, but many dogs remain unvaccinated and continue to spread and succumb to these

The tongue is the major heat dissipating organ of the dog. When it becomes as swollen as this dog's tongue is, the dog should be cooled with damp towels or placed in a cooler area. The ears also dissipate heat, and dampening them can aid in cooling.

off, and vaccinations given before that time are ineffective. So you must revaccinate over a period of weeks so that your pup will not be unprotected and will receive lasting immunity. Your pup's breeder will have given the first vaccinations to your pup before it was old enough to go home with you. Bring all information about your pup's vaccination history to your veterinarian on your first visit so that the pup's vaccination schedule can be maintained. Meanwhile, it is best not to let your pup mingle with strange dogs.

Adults: Although track greyhounds receive vaccinations, it is a good idea to have your greyhound vaccinated again when you bring it home. Many will not have received a rabies vaccination, and your dog will need one regardless in order to comply with state law. You will need to provide yearly boosters throughout your greyhound's life.

Internal Parasite Control

Intestinal worms: When you take your greyhound to be vaccinated, bring along a stool specimen so that your veterinarian can also check for worms. Most puppies do have worms at some point, even pups from the most fastidious breeders. This is because some types of worms become encysted in the dam's body long before she became pregnant; perhaps when she herself was a pup. Here the worms lie dormant and immune from worming until hormonal changes due to her pregnancy cause the worms to be activated, and then they infect her babies. You may be tempted to pick up some worm medication and worm your dog yourself. Don't. Over-the-counter wormers are largely ineffective and often more dangerous than those available through your veterinarian. Left untreated, worms can cause vomiting, diarrhea, dull coat, listlessness, anemia, and death. Some heartworm preventives also prevent most types of

potentially fatal illnesses. Don't let your greyhound be one of them.

Puppies: Puppies receive their dam's immunity through nursing in the first day of life. This is why it is important that a pup's mother be properly immunized before breeding and that the pup be able to nurse from its dam. The immunity gained from the mother will wear off after several weeks, and then the pup will be susceptible to disease unless you provide immunity through vaccinations. The problem is that there is no way to know exactly when this passive immunity will wear intestinal worms, so that if you have a recurring problem in an older dog, the heartworm medicine might help.

Tapeworms tend to plague some dogs throughout their lives. The only prevention is to diligently rid your greyhound of fleas, which transmit tapeworms to dogs. Tapeworms look like moving flat white worms on fresh stools, or may dry up and look like rice grains around the dog's anus. Tapeworms are less harmful to your dog's health than other worms, but can cause irritation around the anus.

Safe dewormers for greyhounds include Vercom Paste, Nemex 2, and Droncit; unsafe dewormers include Task, Dichlorophene, Toluene, DNP, and Telmintic.

Common Misconceptions about Worms

Misconception: a dog that is scooting its rear along the ground has worms. This is seldom the case (except for tapeworms); such a dog more likely has impacted anal sacs.

Misconception: feeding a dog sugar and sweets will give it worms. There are good reasons not to feed a dog sweets, but worms have nothing to do with them.

Misconception: dogs should be regularly wormed every month or so. Dogs should be wormed when, and only when, they have been diagnosed with worms. No worm medication is completely without risk, and it is foolish to use it carelessly.

Heartworms: Heartworms are a deadly parasite carried by mosquitoes. Wherever mosquitoes are present, dogs should be on heartworm preventive. There are several types of heartworm preventives on the market; all are effective, but Filaribits Plus are not recommended for greyhounds (standard Filaribits are fine). If you forget to give the preventive as described, your greyhound may get heartworms. A dog

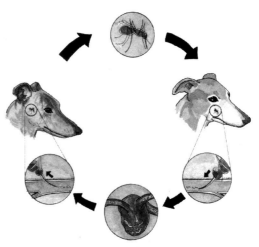

Life cycle of the heartworm. The heartworm enters the dog's body when the dog is bitten by a mosquito that has previously bitten a dog harboring heartworms.

with suspected heartworms should not be given the preventive, because a fatal reaction could occur. Heartworms are treatable in their early stages, but the treatment is expensive and not without risks. If untreated, heartworms will kill your greyhound.

Common Ailments and Symptoms

Coughing

Any persistent cough should be checked by your veterinarian. Coughing irritates the throat and can lead to secondary infections if allowed to continue unchecked. There are many reasons for coughing, including allergies and foreign bodies, but two of the most common are kennel cough and heart disease.

Kennel cough is a highly communicable airborne disease against which your dog can be vaccinated. This is an especially good idea if you plan to have your dog around other dogs at

HOW-TO:
Dealing with Emergencies

Emergencies seldom occur during your veterinarian's office hours. Know the phone number and route to the emergency veterinarian.

Your greyhound's first-aid kit should contain these items:
- rectal thermometer
- scissors
- tweezers
- sterile gauze dressings
- self-adhesive bandage (Vet-Wrap)
- instant cold compress
- antidiarrhea medication
- ophthalmic ointment
- soap
- antiseptic skin ointment
- hydrogen peroxide
- first aid instructions
- veterinarian and emergency clinic numbers.
- poison control number

Deciding whether or not you have an emergency can sometimes be difficult. The following situations are all life-threatening

An emergency muzzle can be fashioned from a strip of cloth or string. Follow the steps clockwise from upper left.

Use a board or blanket to move an injured dog, taking care not to move any injured parts, and to keep the dog as flat as possible.

emergencies. For all cases, administer the first-aid treatment outlined and seek the nearest veterinary help immediately. Call the clinic first so that they can prepare.

In general:
- Be calm and reassuring. A calm dog is less likely to go into shock.
- Move the dog as little and as gently as possible.
- Make sure breathing passages are open. Loosen the collar and check mouth and throat.
- A dog in pain may bite and should be muzzled unless breathing difficulties are present.

Shock
Signs: Very pale gums, weakness, unresponsiveness, faint pulse, shivering.

Treatment: Keep the dog warm and calm; control any bleeding; check breathing, pulse, and consciousness and treat these problems if needed.

Gastric Dilatation/Torsion (Bloat)
Signs: Distended abdomen, restlessness, panting, salivation, attempts to vomit.

Treatment: Get the dog to the veterinarian immediately. Survival is directly related to promptness of treatment. The twisted stomach cuts off the blood supply to tissues, resulting in tissue death that may ultimately cause the dog's death. Passing a tube into the stomach to release gas may help as a preliminary measure in some cases.

Heat Stroke
Signs: Rapid, loud breathing; abundant thick saliva, bright red mucous membranes, high rectal temperature. Later signs: unsteadiness, diarrhea, coma.

Treatment: Immediately cover the dog in towels soaked in cold water and place it in a cold area or in front of a fan. If this is not possible gradually immerse the dog in water. If rectal temperature is extremely high—over 106°F (41.1°C)—give a water enema. You must lower your dog's body temperature quickly, but do not lower it below 100°F (37.8°C).

Breathing Difficulties
Signs: Gasping for breath with head extended, anxiety, weakness; advances to loss of consciousness, bluish tongue (Exception: carbon monoxide poisoning causes bright red tongue).

Treatment: If the dog is not breathing, give mouth-to-nose respiration:

If emergency is due to drowning, turn dog upside down, holding it by its stomach area, so that water can run out of its mouth. Then administer mouth-to-nose respiration, with the dog's head positioned lower than its lungs.

1. Open dog's mouth, clear passage of secretions and foreign bodies.
2. Pull dog's tongue forward.
3. Seal your mouth over dog's nose and mouth, blow gently into dog's nose for three seconds, then release.
4. Continue until dog breathes on its own.

Poisoning

Signs: Vary according to poison, but commonly include vomiting, convulsions, staggering, collapse.

Treatment: Call your veterinarian and give as much information as possible. Induce vomiting (except in the cases listed in the next paragraph) by giving either hydrogen peroxide, salt water, or mustard and water. Treat for shock and get to the veterinarian at once. Be prepared for convulsions or respiratory distress.

Do not induce vomiting if the poison was an acid, alkali, petroleum product, solvent, cleaner, tranquilizer, or if a sharp object was swallowed; also do not induce vomiting if the dog is severely depressed, convulsing, comatose, or if over two hours have passed since ingestion. If the dog is not convulsing or unconscious: dilute the poison by giving milk, vegetable oil, or egg whites.

Convulsions

Signs: Drooling, stiffness, muscle spasms.

Treatment: Prevent the dog from injuring itself on furniture or stairs. Remove other dogs from area. Treat for shock.

Snakebites

Signs: Swelling, discoloration, pain, fang marks, restlessness, nausea, weakness.

Treatment: Restrain the dog and keep it quiet. Be able to describe the snake. If you can't get to the veterinarian, apply a tourniquet between the bite and the heart tight enough to prevent blood's returning to the heart. Make vertical parallel cuts (deep enough for blood to ooze out) through the fang marks and suction out the blood. Do not use your mouth if you have any open sores.

Open Wounds

Signs: Consider a wound to be an emergency if there is profuse bleeding, if the wound is extremely deep, if it is open to the chest cavity, or abdominal cavity, or head.

Treatment: Control massive bleeding first. Cover the wound with clean dressing and apply pressure; apply more dressings over the others until bleeding stops. Also elevate the wound site and apply a cold pack to the site.

If the wound is on an extremity, apply pressure to the closest pressure point as follows:
• For a front leg: inside of front leg just above the elbow.
• For a rear leg: inside of thigh where the femoral artery crosses the thighbone.
• For the tail: underside of tail close to where it joins the body.
Note: With open wounds, use a tourniquet only in life-threatening situations and when all other attempts have failed. Check for signs of shock.

Sucking chest wounds: Place sheet of plastic or other nonporous material over the hole and bandage it to make an airtight seal.

Abdominal wounds: Place warm, wet, sterile dressing over any protruding internal organs; cover with bandage or towel. Do not attempt to push organs back into the dog.

Head wounds: Apply gentle pressure to control bleeding. Monitor for loss of consciousness or shock and treat accordingly.

Deep Burns

Signs: Charred or pearly white skin; deeper layers of tissue exposed.

Treatment: Cool the burned area with cool packs, towels soaked in ice water, or by immersing in cold water. If over 50 percent of the dog is burned, do not immerse, as this increases likelihood of shock. Cover with clean bandage or towel to avoid contamination. Do not apply pressure; do not apply ointments. Monitor for shock.

Electrical Shock

Signs: Collapse, burns inside mouth.

Treatment: Before touching the dog, disconnect electric plug or cut power; if that cannot be done immediately, use a wooden pencil, spoon, or broom handle to knock cord away from the dog. Keep the dog warm and treat for shock. Monitor breathing and heartbeat.

Note: The foregoing is not a complete catalog of emergency situations. Situations not described can usually be treated with the same first aid as for humans. In all cases follow emergency treatment with veterinary care.

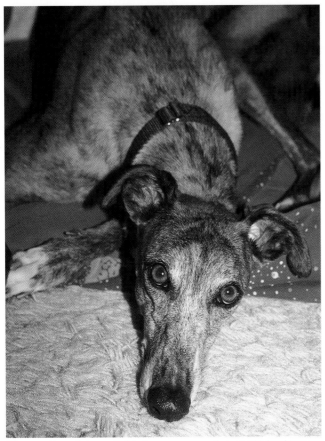

Your greyhound depends totally upon you and your veterinarian to care for its health needs.

A collapsed trachea may cause coughing, especially following running. In these dogs the rings of the trachea are not formed correctly, and the upper part of the trachea may collapse inward during heavy breathing. Rubbing the area beneath the neck or use of a tight collar may also cause coughing. The condition may be corrected surgically.

Vomiting

Vomiting is a not uncommon occurrence that may or may not indicate a serious problem. You should consult your veterinarian immediately if your dog vomits a foul substance resembling fecal matter (indicating a blockage in the intestinal tract), blood (partially digested blood resembles coffee grounds), or if there is projectile vomiting, in which the stomach contents are forcibly ejected up to a distance of several feet. Sporadic vomiting with poor appetite and generally poor condition could indicate worms or a more serious internal disease that should also be checked by your veterinarian.

Attempts to vomit, usually without success, accompanied by distended abdomen and restlessness, may indicate gastric dilatation (bloat). See HOW-TO: Dealing with Emergencies (page 62).

Persistent vomiting of undigested food soon after eating may indicate esophageal achalasia, a condition that is seen in some greyhounds in which food is prevented from entering the stomach.

Vomiting after eating grass is common and usually of no great concern. But repeated vomiting could indicate that the dog has eaten spoiled food, undigestible objects, or may have stomach illness. If vomiting is repeated, continues for a second day, or is accompanied by general malaise, seek veterinary advice. For mild vomit-

training classes or while being boarded. If your dog has a sudden gagging cough, especially about eight days after being around other dogs, it may have kennel cough. Do not take your dog into the veterinarian's waiting room to infect all of the other dogs.

Heart disease can result in coughing following exercise or in the evening. Treatment with diuretics prescribed by your veterinarian can help alleviate the coughing for awhile. Heartworms can also cause coughing in advanced stages.

ing, use the same home treatment as that outlined for diarrhea.

Diarrhea

Diarrhea can result from overexcitement or nervousness, a change in diet or water, sensitivity to certain foods, overeating, intestinal parasites, infectious diseases such as parvovirus or corona virus, or ingestion of toxic substances. Bloody diarrhea, diarrhea with vomiting, fever, or other signs of toxicity, or diarrhea that lasts for more than a day should not be allowed to continue without veterinary advice.

Less severe diarrhea can be treated at home by withholding or severely restricting food and water. Ice cubes can be given to satisfy thirst. Administer a human antidiarrheal medicine (Immodium) in the same weight dosage as recommended for humans. A bland diet consisting of rice (flavored if need be with cooked, drained hamburger), cottage cheese, or cooked macaroni should be given for several days.

Chronic loose stools may be improved by adjusting the fat percentage in the diet. A fat content of 15 percent has been found to result in firm stools in greyhounds.

Urinary Tract Diseases

If your greyhound drinks and urinates more than usual, it may be suffering from a kidney problem. See your veterinarian for a proper diagnosis and treatment. Although the excessive urination may cause problems in keeping your house clean or your night's sleep intact, never try to restrict water for a dog with kidney disease. Untreated kidney disease can lead to death. Increased thirst and urination could also be a sign of diabetes.

If your dog has difficulty or pain in urination, urinates suddenly but in small amounts, or passes cloudy or bloody urine, it may be suffering from a problem of the bladder, urethra, or prostate. Your veterinarian will need to examine your greyhound to determine the exact nature of the problem. Bladder infections must be treated promptly to avoid the infection's reaching the kidneys. A common cause of urinary incontinence in older spayed females is lack of estrogen, which can be treated. Your veterinarian should check your older male's prostate to ensure that it is not overly enlarged, which can cause problems in both urination and defecation.

Older males may have an infection of the penis sheath, indicated by dribbling a thick greenish substance, and by constant licking of the area. Older females can develop urine scald or vaginitis. Both require veterinary attention.

Impacted Anal Sacs

Dogs have two anal sacs that are normally emptied by rectal pressure during defecation. Their musky-smelling contents may also be forcibly ejected when a dog is extremely frightened. Sometimes they fail to empty properly and become impacted or infected. Constant licking of the anus or "scooting" along the ground are characteristic signs of anal sac impaction. Not only is this an extremely uncomfortable condition for your dog, but left unattended, the impacted sacs can become infected. Your veterinarian can show you how to empty the anal sacs yourself. Some dogs may never need to have their anal sacs expressed, but others may need regular attention.

Eye Disorders

A watery discharge, accompanied by squinting or pawing, often indicates a foreign body in the eye. Examine under the lids and use a moist cotton swab to remove any debris. Flooding the eye with saline solution (such as that used for contact lenses) can also aid in removal.

Tape a hollow, well-ventilated hair curler over the tip of a damaged tail.

are frequently damaged from excessive wagging and hitting on walls and furniture. Fractures should be set by your veterinarian; during the healing period wagging should be prevented by tying a bandage from the tail tip to the hock. Damaged tail tips can be treated in the same fashion, but if the bone is exposed the tail tip may need to be amputated. Taping a hollow hair curler around the tip will both protect it and allow air to circulate during the healing process.

Continued watering without pain may indicate a blocked tear duct. A thick or crusty discharge suggests conjunctivitis. Your veterinarian can treat both of these conditions.

Pannus is a progressive disease seen in some greyhounds in which blood vessels grow over and cloud the cornea (the normally clear outer layer of the eye). Avoid sun exposure and see your veterinarian if pannus is suspected.

Some greyhounds develop retinal atrophy, a possibly hereditary condition in which the visual nerve cells of the eye gradually deteriorate. It is noticed at around one to three years of age, and progresses to blindness. Dogs may lose interest in chasing, and have an increased "eyeshine." There is no treatment.

Any time your dog's pupils do not react to light or when one eye reacts differently from another, take the dog to the veterinarian immediately. It could indicate a serious ocular or neurological problem.

Tale of the Tail

Greyhound tails are frequently broken through door encounters, and tips

Limping

Limping due to injuries is covered in the Greyhound Fitness chapter (page 70).

Unfortunately, another cause of lameness is bone cancer. The growth can occur on any bone, and its incidence increases with increasing age. Bone cancer is prevalent in any large breed, but seems to occur with more than average frequency in greyhounds. It typically involves limping or pain along with a bony tumor. Treatment may require amputation of a limb, and you will want to discuss your dog's prognosis earnestly with your veterinarian before undertaking such a step.

Skin Problems

Greyhounds are far less prone to skin problems than most breeds, and are rarely plagued with skin allergies. Greyhounds are somewhat prone to staphylococcal infections, especially if kept in dirty conditions or with external parasites. These infections are characterized by multiple pus-filled blisters and scabs; cure requires extreme cleanliness usually combined with antibiotics.

See under Greyhound Maintenance (page 46) for a discussion of other skin problems.

Greyhound Fitness

Greyhounds are born to run. To deprive them of the chance to push their bodies to the limit, to run faster than they ran the day before, is to deprive them of their life's essence. Most greyhound owners find that the opportunity to observe one of nature's most graceful creations racing the wind is a high point of living with a greyhound. But whenever an animal covers ground at such a high rate of speed it runs an increased risk of injury and accidents, so it is your job to ensure that your greyhound satisfies its need for exercise safely. You can do this by gradual conditioning, careful choice of exercise locales, and prompt attention to minor injuries.

Conditioning

Most ex-racing greyhounds arrive preconditioned; that is, if they are fresh off the track and have not been injured, they are probably already in very good athletic shape. A greyhound that has been injured, however, will need to rebuild itself gradually before being allowed to blast off at even a fraction of Mach speed. Swimming and walking are an excellent beginning.

Swimming is the best exercise for injured dogs, but not all greyhounds are eager water dogs. To teach your greyhound to swim, ease it into the water gradually, and get right in there beside it. Elevate the dog's hindquarters when it is first learning to swim; this will help it to quit thrashing with its front feet above the water. Eventually your greyhound can become a skilled—and perhaps enthusiastic—swimmer.

Walking is the next best choice for a recovering dog, and much more practical for most owners. For decades, walking was the traditional conditioning regime for the highly successful racing greyhounds in Europe. Many a local lad supplemented the family income by walking groups of greyhounds for miles, often twice a day.

Walking a greyhound can bring tranquillity, but it can also end in aggravation, because, as with anything else, there is a right way, and a wrong way, to do it. If you are walking around the neighborhood, use a collar that will not slip over your greyhound's head, a 6-foot (2m) nonchain leash, or a longer retractable leash. Hold the leash firmly, keep your eyes open for marauding canines and enticing felines, and never allow so much loose lead that your dog could suddenly jump into the path

Greyhounds love to be chased in a friendly game of tag.

A dog that pulls a lot can wear a harness for walking. Note that the pricked ears of this ex-racer, seen in some dogs as an indication of extreme excitement, is nonetheless a faulty trait by AKC standards—but in no way interferes with this lucky dog's ability to function as a beautiful walking companion.

of a passing vehicle. An astounding number of dogs get hit by cars while on lead because their owners neglect to be prepared for the unexpected. It is not advisable to have young children walk a greyhound, because a child may not be able to hold the dog back if the dog decides it's off to the races!

Keep up a brisk pace, and work up to longer distances. A greyhound should walk at the very least a half mile daily, and would prefer to walk several miles. Walking is an excellent low-impact exercise for recovering and elderly dogs, but the drawbacks are that it takes a long time and does not develop the muscles of the back and loin. Unless your dog has a permanent injury, eventually you will want to integrate other activities into your dog's exercise schedule.

Greyhounds can make good jogging companions if they are worked up to longer distances gradually. The greyhound is a natural athlete, but athletes need conditioning, and there are different types of athletes. The greyhound, especially the NGA greyhound, is a sprinter, not a long-distance runner. Marathon jogs may not be your greyhound's idea of fun. When jogging any distance, monitor your greyhound for signs of fatigue or overheating. Leave your dog at home in hot weather. Dogs are unable to cool themselves through sweating, and heatstroke in jogging dogs is unfortunately a common emergency seen by veterinarians in the summer. Check the foot pads regularly for signs of abrasion, foreign bodies, tears, or blistering from hot pavement. Track greyhounds have run only on

Contrary to some owner's opinions, greyhounds cannot walk on water—but they can run on it!

sand and have tender pads. Never ask a puppy to jog to the point of fatigue; puppies should set their own limits and can be injured by being required to exceed them.

Of course, there are far lazier ways to jog your dog. Some people will roadwork their dogs, often beside a bicycle. This requires a dog trained to trot steadily without pulling, a tall order if there are loose cats and dogs in the neighborhood. Roadwork beside a car is asking for trouble. Roadwork can be a good alternative if a safe place is available and you are short on time, but it can result in spills for the owner and other assorted mishaps. Besides, it still doesn't condition the whole dog. Running at a full double-suspension gallop is the only way to condition the powerful muscles of the loin, but in order to do that, you will need to find a greyhound-safe field.

Safety Afield

Your greyhound and you may both dream of open spaces where the two

of you can frolic joyously and share an adventurous odyssey. In most areas, this may have to remain a fantasy, but with some effort you should be able to find a safe place to let your greyhound run at full tilt. Never allow your greyhound to run loose in sight of traffic, even if that traffic is a mere speck in the distance. A greyhound can travel a startling distance in only a few seconds. Remember that the greyhound was bred to chase first and ask questions later!

Although your dog may usually stay with you, keep in mind that a cat, rabbit, or other dogs can lure your dog away (or even scare it away) and cause it to end up in potentially dangerous places. Never unhook the lead until you know everything about the area in which you will be walking. Is there a roadway around the next bend in the path? Dogs have been killed or injured running off unseen cliffs, carried away by fast moving water in drainage culverts, and even eaten by alligators. Watch out for

HOW-TO:
Dealing with Running Injuries

Because greyhounds consider running to be the very essence of being, they have a tendency to do so with far too little regard for their own well-being. This, combined with the anatomical fact that they have extremely powerful musculature propelling long, relatively thin bones at a high rate of speed, provides the perfect recipe for a myriad of limps and lumps.

The most common injuries are those involving the feet, and any lame dog should immediately have its feet examined for burrs, cuts, peeled pads, or misaligned toes. Cuts and peeled pads should be carefully

One method of wrapping an injured foot is to begin near the toes with the Vet-Wrap wrapping around the leg at a 45 degree angle to the ground, so that it crosses over itself and clings better. Use a strip of adhesive tape to anchor it in position at the top and bottom of the wrap.

flushed with warm water, and have an antibacterial ointment applied. Cover the area with gauze, then wrap the foot with Vet-Wrap. Change the dressing daily and restrict exercise until it heals. If you need a quick fix for a minor injury, you can fashion a makeshift pad by adhering a thin piece of leather or rubber to the bottom of the pad with Super-Glue, or you can apply a coat of Nu-Skin (available at drug stores) if the injury is not too extensive. A local anesthetic such as hemorrhoid cream or a topical toothache salve can help ease discomfort. Deep cuts should be checked by your veterinarian for foreign objects or for tendon damage.

Split or broken nails can be treated by cutting the nail as short as possible and soaking it in warm salt water. Apply an antibiotic and then a human fingernail mender, followed by a bandage.

A deep cut directly above and behind the foot may sever the tendons to the toes, causing them to lose their arch. Immediate veterinary attention should be sought, but even that may not help.

If the webbing between the toes is split, it will continue to split further. This is another condition that warrants a trip to the vet.

A "jammed toe" results from the stubbing of a toe on a root, rock, or other hard surface. A toe that is simply bruised will improve with rest, but any toe injury is potentially serious. In severe cases a toe may have to be amputated to avoid persistent lameness. Many ex-racers

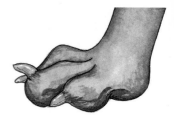

One of several toe problems, known among greyhound trainers as a "dropped toe." Note that one toe has a flattened arch and raised toenail. Another condition, the "popped up toe" has the raised toenail without the flattened arch. These conditions result from different ligaments being torn.

arrive with a previous history of toe problems.

Occasionally an outside toe will be displaced from its joint and stick out to the side of the foot. This causes extreme pain for the dog, and although it would be preferable to have your veterinarian fix it, when your dog is screaming you will want to try something yourself. Pull the toe gently forward and allow it to go back into its proper position. Wrap the foot in Vet-Wrap, totally restrict exercise, and seek veterinary attention. Toes that become dislocated often have stretched or torn ligaments, and the problem will tend to recur and then worsen with each subsequent dislocation. Keeping the nail of the affected toe trimmed as short as possible may help, but surgery, or possibly amputation, may be needed for a complete recovery. If the entire foot sticks out to the side, it may be a dislocated wrist, which should receive prompt veterinary attention.

In general, if a toe is swollen, does not match its fellow toe on the opposite foot in shape and position, or makes a grinding sound if moved, or if the dog shows considerable pain when the toe is manipulated, the toe should be immobilized and checked by your veterinarian. Meanwhile minimize swelling by applying cold packs or placing the extremity in a bucket of cold water.

The most common nonfoot injuries are muscle injuries. These usually cause little lameness but pronounced swelling, or can be felt as a hole in the muscle. Torn muscles may need surgery for a complete recovery, but all muscle injuries should be treated with an initial ice pack followed by at least one week's rest.

A good rule of thumb for any mild lameness is to rest the dog completely for three days; if the lameness persists, see the veterinarian.

An all too common source of hind leg lameness in most large breeds of dogs is a ruptured cruciate ligament. This ligament holds the stifle joint (knee) from wobbling side to side. Although the injury may seem to get better with rest, the dog will be lame again as soon as it is allowed to run. This injury will not get better on its own, and should be treated surgically.

Any time that a dog is lame and also exhibits swelling or deformation of the affected leg, it could indicate a break or

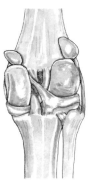

The stifle, or knee joint, is stabilized by several cruciate ligaments. If one of the ligaments is torn, the joint becomes unstable and the floating, loose ligament causes pain when the dog walks or runs. Surgical correction involves removing the torn pieces and stabilizing the joint with wire or an artificial ligament.

another serious problem. Any suspected break should be immobilized and taken for immediate veterinary attention.

Aspirin or other prescription medications can alleviate some of the discomfort, but never give them if your dog is on its way for possible surgery. If you administer pain medication you must confine your greyhound, preferably in a cage or X-pen. Although you don't want your dog to be in pain, pain prevents your dog from using the affected limb, which would cause it further damage.

Occasionally a greyhound will run into something, usually as a result of looking sideways while running straight ahead, or by not being able to turn sharply

enough when running full speed. Resulting injuries could range from broken bones to a collapsed lung to death, but the dog could also emerge unhurt. It would be advisable to have your veterinarian check your dog after any such collision, and certainly rest your dog for a few days.

The foregoing is but a sample of the injuries that greyhounds can sustain. The greyhound owner has one large advantage over the owner of other dog breeds: an immense amount of knowledge exists about lameness in greyhounds, as a result of the racing greyhound industry. Veterinary orthopedists are especially well-versed in greyhound anatomy and may prove helpful in stubborn cases. If you have a problem, make every effort to find an orthopedist or a veterinarian who works on racing greyhounds. The key feature in any recovery, however, is rest, rest, and more rest.

Some people become so worried that their dog will injure itself that they seldom, or never, let it run. But injuries are not that common, and a dog that runs only rarely will be more likely to injure itself because it is not in condition, it lacks the experience necessary to learn how to control its body at high speeds, and it is so filled with exuberance at the chance to finally run that it often does so to excess. In the greyhound's mind it is better to have run and to have been hurt (a little) than never to have run at all.

Slamming on the brakes, a greyhound runs over the lure as it slows at the end of a course.

strange dogs; some may not be friendly and may chase your greyhound away or start a fight. Greyhounds are poor fighters and their thin fur makes them extremely vulnerable to injury. Watch too that your greyhound does not present a danger to small dogs or other domestic animals running loose that your dog might mistake as prey objects.

An area chock-full of small game, such as squirrels and rabbits, may seem like greyhound utopia, but can be a dangerous choice. Although each individual squirrel may not run far, if there is always another just a little farther away, your greyhound can disappear while chasing one after another. Even more dangerous is an area filled with deer. Greyhounds find them irresistible and may chase them for great distances, perhaps getting lost or hit by a car in the process. In most states it is illegal for a dog to chase deer.

You must also beware of hunters; a greyhound at a distance can be mistaken for a deer and shot. It is always best to have your dog wear a bright jacket, such as those used in lure-coursing competition, when running in the field. This both helps the hunter realize this is not a masquerading deer and helps you spot a wanderer at a distance.

Once you know your area is safe be prepared to enjoy a breathtaking spectacle, as this most perfect of canines uses every muscle and sinew to achieve an unrivaled mixture of grace and power. Seen from a distance the greyhound seems almost to float weightlessly across the ground, but as it approaches you this illusion is belied by the rumble of the earth from its pounding footfalls. Just be sure to stand perfectly still (and perhaps give a shout or wave your arms); a collision

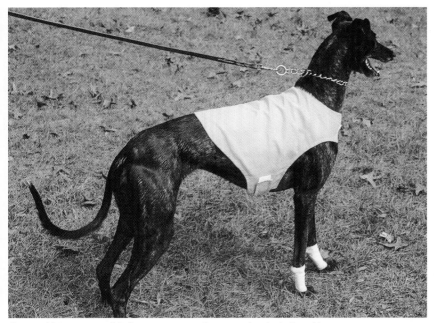

Dressed for success, this top courser sports a coursing jacket and leg wraps.

with a 40-miles-per-hour (64.372 km/hr) greyhound is seriously dangerous for both human and dog. The flyby is a favorite greyhound game; they seem to achieve an almost perverse delight in seeing how close they can whiz by and barely miss you.

Greyhounds have their own set of games. Many new owners are dismayed to find that their greyhound will not retrieve a ball, catch a frisbee, or swim after a stick. These simply are not greyhound games. Greyhound games involve high-speed running; greyhounds basically like to chase or be chased. Tag is a big favorite, but you might as well know: you will always be "it" and you can't win against a greyhound! Of course, they'll let you get close enough so that you'll keep on playing, but if there is one expression that captures the feeling of pure ecstasy, it is the look on your greyhound's face as you once again lunge but just can't quite tag it!

You may worry that with such joy your dog may be overcome with the call of the wild and run away. Probably not. But for insurance you should practice letting your greyhound run loose in enclosed areas such as ball fields, practice the "come" command, and use treats to ensure that your dog comes every single time. Practice having your dog come to you and then let it run again, so that it does not associate returning to you with relinquishing its freedom. You may even want to make sure that your dog is already hungry (and maybe a little tired) before the run if you have any doubts about its eager return. If you ever do have a situation where your dog is loose and ignoring your command to come, it is handy to have a lure with you (a white plastic bag on a string; see coursing section, page 75). Whatever you do,

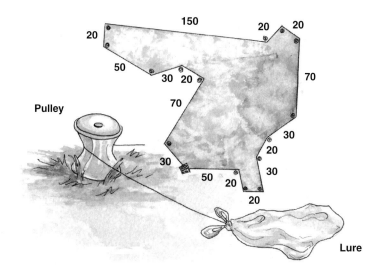

In lure-coursing, the lure is pulled through a field along a string that is looped around several pulleys. The sample course design shown here tests the dogs' speed, agility, and endurance.

don't chase your greyhound! You will never catch it (remember that tag game?), and it will think it has discovered a wonderful new way to lead you wherever it wants to go. If you have a car, get into it and act as if you're driving away. It's amazing how obedient errant dogs become at this sight!

Most sighthounds are independent (although greyhounds are not as independent as some others) and many people are reluctant to ever let them run free. This will have to be your personal decision. It does seem, however, that the dogs that have never experienced freedom are the ones that run out of control and become lost when they accidentally do get loose.

When running your dog, pack some water and a little bowl for your dog, as well as tape and bandages in case of a cut foot pad. There may, in fact, be recreation that greyhounds like better than running; however, it has yet to be discovered—that is, unless you count coursing.

Coursing, of Course

Dogs innately love to do what they were bred to do, and greyhounds were bred to chase game, or course. Greyhounds absolutely love to course, whether the real thing or make-believe. The real thing is live game (or "open field") coursing, with competitions in the United States sponsored by the National Open Field Coursing Association (NOFCA), but open field coursing is limited to states where jackrabbits abound; besides, because it often involves the killing of live game and an entire day of walking in the field, it is decidedly not for everyone.

For the greyhound, and most greyhound owners, the thrill is in the chase, not the kill. Thus, most greyhounds will chase a simulated quarry with every bit as much gusto as they will live game.

The sport of lure-coursing was developed to simulate live coursing without killing any animals, walking all day, coping with the dangers of the open field, or trying to judge hounds running game over dissimilar courses. Instead, a white plastic bag is dragged at high speed by way of a pulley system placed on the ground in a large field. Greyhounds go wild at the sight! Even dogs that have never seen a live rabbit, or have never been trained to run, instinctively want to chase the lure. Retired racers are especially eager and adept, although initially have some difficulty negotiating the sharp turns that they had never seen on the track.

Dogs are scored not only on their speed, but also their agility, endurance, enthusiasm, and how well they follow the lure. (Some wise guys try to outsmart it by cutting corners and lying in wait!) Some ex-racers that weren't quite fast enough to gain fame on the track have done so in the coursing field, where the best is not necessarily the fastest. Both NGA and AKC greyhounds compete successfully in lure-coursing.

Coursing more closely simulates the job that the ancient greyhound was bred to perform. The sight of the dogs using all of their immense physical attributes to hurtle at blinding speed over a zigzag course is truly awe-inspiring and must explain in part both the ancient and modern fascination with this oldest of sports.

If you are attending your first lure-course with your greyhound, a word of advice: Hold on tight! Many people cannot believe how excited their usually dignified hounds become at the sight of a white trash bag being dragged around a field. And more than a few have found themselves dragged across the field behind an overly zealous and powerful greyhound. If you don't believe it, try this little experiment: tie a white plastic trash bag to a six-foot (2m) string, and tie the other end of the string to a six-foot (2m) stick. Run around your yard dragging it erratically (while your next-door neigh-

bors are away, of course) and watch your greyhound react! Playing keep-away with this "pole-lure" is another very favorite greyhound game.

In many breeds dogs tend to try to play with each other when given a chance to chase the lure together. Dogs that repeatedly interfere with their running partners are usually required to be retrained before entering a field trial. Luckily, greyhounds very seldom interfere with each other, being too single-minded for the chase to even notice another dog on the field.

Both the AKC and the American Sighthound Field Association (ASFA) sponsor lure-coursing field trials and award titles: the AKC awards the suffixes Junior Courser (JC) for a dog that demonstrates it can complete a course running alone, Senior Courser (SC) for dogs that demonstrate they can also complete a course running alongside two other dogs, and the prefix Field Champion (FCH) for dogs that win against competition in a number of trials. The ASFA also awards the FCH title (but as a suffix) for dogs that win at several trials over competition, and goes on to award the suffix Lure Courser of Merit (LCM) for continued success against other Field Champions. Contact the AKC or the ASFA for a rule book and a list of clubs in your area.

Simply because your dog is not AKC-registered does not mean you won't be able to run it competitively. ASFA recognizes NGA registration, as well as AKC and AKC-indefinite listing privilege (ILP) numbers. An ILP number can be obtained from AKC even without NGA registration; the number is granted to a dog with evidence of purebreeding so that it may compete in obedience and field trials, but ILP does not constitute registration for breeding or conformation showing purposes. Dogs must be spayed or neutered to receive an ILP number.

A slip lead is used to release the dog when coursing. By letting go with the right hand, the entire leash and collar will fall away from the dog.

Regular AKC registration is available to all NGA registered greyhounds (request an application to register a dog registered with another domestic registry). You must first transfer the NGA registration to your name, which can be difficult because it is often impossible to locate the dog's former official owners.

Some owners are reluctant to try lure-coursing because they fear the possibility of injuries. This fear is not without foundation, but there is much you can do to lessen the probability. First, if your greyhound is an ex-racer, find out why it was retired. If retirement was due to a serious racing injury, ask your veterinarian or the greyhound adoption agency if they believe hard running could reinjure the dog. For a greyhound, there is no such thing as halfway. Once you let the dog loose after the lure, it will not run at half-speed or run half the distance; it is all or nothing. Make sure your dog is physically fit and sound of limb or do not let it run the lure at all. Injuries are far more likely to occur in dogs that are not in shape. Always limber your dog up before running,

and walk it afterwards. Your greyhound is an athlete and should be treated as such.

If the weather is warm, bring water in which to soak your dog both before and after running. Greyhounds do not handle running in hot weather as well as some other breeds, and it may be best to skip running on a very hot day. At a trial your dog will be required to run at least two courses, and there will be the option of running more if the dog wins and then competes against other winners toward the ultimate Best In Field. But you may and should quit at any time that your dog appears overheated, sore, or lame. Recall that a racing greyhound is asked to run only about 5/16 of a mile (about .5 km) at most once every three days.

Most courses are set up in clear fields without obstructions, but some are laid out in fields with a few trees. It is the duty of the club to design a course that is safe for all dogs, but if your dog is fresh off the track, it may not expect or know how to negotiate sharp turns such as those seen in lure-coursing. Thus, expect it to overshoot the turns at high speed at its first few trials, and examine the course layout carefully to ensure that there are no obstacles anywhere that an overshooting dog could hit. If you have concerns, voice them to the Field Chairman; if they are not met, pull your dog from competition and go home. The number one concern at any field trial should be safety.

Most greyhound injuries in lure-coursing involve the feet, and are usually minor. Most common is peeling the large pad. You can avoid this to some extent by using a pad conditioner (Tuff Foot) or wrapping the rear part of the foot with Vet-Wrap (a miracle leg wrap that clings to itself and can be found at most horse supply stores, some pet stores, and veterinary clinics). In fact, you should wrap the front feet up to and including the stop pad at the rear of the pastern, as this, too, is often peeled. Of course, make sure your dog is not wrapped so much that it looks (and walks) like a mummy!

Another fear that owners have about lure-coursing is that it will awaken some primordial urge to kill and render their greyhound a rabid beast unfit to live around cats and small dogs. But most track greyhounds have already had the chase instinct developed to its highest possible degree. Any greyhound owner should exercise caution when allowing a greyhound to run loose around potential prey animals, whether it has been coursed or not. A scurrying cat is a lot more likely to awaken buried instincts than is a plastic bag!

Coursing is undeniably more dangerous than snoozing on the couch, but it also has several major attributes that set it apart from other organized greyhound activities. For one, it is the best way to test greyhounds in a way that most closely simulates the job for

Both greyhound and owner can get a lot of exercise (and fun) by playing with the pole lure in the backyard.

which they were bred. For another, it is populated by very nice pet-owning people who appreciate watching a beautiful dog turn in a beautiful course, and are eager to welcome and help others who want to share this experience. Because the dog is the one being judged, it is an area of competition where a novice owner can win as readily as a veteran. Finally, if your greyhound could talk it would say: "Let's do it!"

To Train a Greyhound

A breed that has been selected to chase without question or human direction should not be a good candidate to graduate with honors from an obedience class. But the angelic and easygoing nature of greyhounds makes them surprisingly easy to train as long as it's done gently. Most training classes are geared toward the boisterous hard-to-control dog. They emphasize repetition and means by which to dominate and calm these dogs. Greyhounds are already calm. They will learn the "Down-Stay" before any other dog in the class. But they will also learn to be bored and to lag behind while heeling before any other dog in the class. Whether you want an obedience star or a well-mannered pet, there are certain concepts that a

Correct placement of the choke collar.

every good trainer should know, and certain commands that every good greyhound should know.

What Every Good Greyhound Trainer Should Know

Successful greyhound trainers all emphasize that greyhounds must be trained with an extremely light hand, with lots of positive reinforcement in the form of praise, food, or toys, and virtually no corrections or repetitions of exercises. Remember the following rules of greyhound training:

Gently guide: Greyhounds want to please but don't want to be ordered. Tough, domineering training techniques are improper for greyhounds. You don't have to show them who's boss—they have already elected you.

Name first: The first ingredient in any command is your dog's name. You probably spend a good deal of your day talking, with very few words intended as commands for your dog. So warn your greyhound that this talk is directed toward it.

Then command: Many trainers make the mistake of saying the command word at the same time that they are placing the dog into position. This is incorrect. The command comes immediately before the desired action or position. The crux of training is anticipation: the dog comes to anticipate that after hearing a command, it will be induced to perform some action, and it will eventually perform this action without further assistance from you. On the other hand, when the command and action come at the same time, not only does the dog tend to pay more attention to your action of placing it in position, and less attention to the command word, but the command word loses its predictive value for the dog. Remember: Name, command, action!

Once is enough: Repeating a word over and over, or shouting it louder and louder, never helped anyone, dog or human, to understand what is expected. Your greyhound is not hard-of-hearing.

Say what you mean and mean what you say: Your greyhound takes its commands literally. If you have taught that "Down" means to lie down, then what must the dog think when you yell "Down" to tell it to get off the sofa where it was already lying down? If "Stay" means not to move until given a release word, and you say "Stay here" as you leave the house for work, do you really want your dog to sit by the door all day until you get home?

Think like a dog: In many ways dogs are like young children; they act to gratify themselves, and they often do so without regard to consequences. But unlike young children, dogs cannot understand human language (except for those words you teach them), so you cannot explain to them that their actions of five minutes earlier were bad. Dogs live in the present; if you punish them they can only assume it is for their behavior at the time of punishment. So if you discover a mess, drag your dog to it from its nap in the other room, and scold, the dog's impression will be that either it is being scolded for napping, or that its owner is mentally unstable. Remember timing is everything in a correction. If you discover your dog in the process of having an "accident," snatch the dog up and deposit it outside, and then yell "No," your dog can conclude only that you have yelled "No" to it for eliminating outside. Correct timing would be "No," quickly take the dog outside, and then praise it once it eliminates outside. In

It is easier to teach a greyhound to sit by pushing up and back under its chin rather than the traditional method of pulling its neck up by a collar.

this way you have corrected the dog's undesired behavior and helped the dog understand desired behavior.

Correct and be done with it: Owners sometimes try to make this "a correction the dog will remember" by ignoring the dog for the rest of the day. The dog may indeed remember that its owner ignored it, but it will not remember why. Again, the dog can only relate its present behavior to your actions.

Never rough: Such methods as striking, shaking, choking and hanging have been touted by some (stupid) trainers: Do not try them! They are extremely dangerous, counterproductive and cruel; they have no place in the training of a beloved family member. Greyhounds are a sensitive breed both mentally and physically and seldom require anything but the mildest of corrections. A direct stare with a harsh "NO!" should be all that is required in most cases.

Training should be fun! Use whatever your greyhound likes as a reward: praise, tidbits, toys, or even a thrown ball.

Food is forever: There is nothing wrong with using food as a reward *as long as you intend to continue using it throughout the dog's life.* If you train a dog using food to tell it that it has done well, and then quit rewarding it with food, the dog's impression is that it has no longer done well. It may eventually quit performing altogether under these circumstances. If you do use food, precede it with praise; that is, praise, then give a tidbit. On the other hand, don't reward with food every time; keep the dog wondering if this will be the time with the tidbit payoff (the slot machine philosophy of dog training). That way, when you can't reward with a tidbit, your greyhound will not be surprised and will continue to perform in the absence of food for comparatively long periods. Of course, the advantage of using praise rather than food is that you never can be caught without praise available.

Too much of a good thing: There is such a thing as overpraising a dog throughout the day. Think of it this way: if you spend the day praising and petting your greyhound just for breathing, why should it work for your praise later when it can get it for free? Certainly you should praise, pet, and love your greyhound, but in some cases of disobedience such "handouts" must be curtailed. Such overindulged greyhounds must learn the value of praise by earning it.

Be consistent: Sometimes a greyhound can be awfully cute when it misbehaves, or sometimes your hands are full, and sometimes you just aren't sure what you want from your dog. But lapses in consistency are ultimately unfair to the dog. If you feed your begging greyhound from the table "just this one time," you have taught it that while begging may not always result in a handout, you never know, it just might

There is a myth that greyhounds are physically unable to sit. Judge for yourself!

pay off tonight. In other words, you have taught your dog to beg.

Train before meals: Your dog will work better if its stomach is not full, and will be more responsive to treats if you use them as rewards. Never try to train a sleepy, tired, or hot greyhound.

Happy endings: Begin and end each training session with something the dog can do well. And keep sessions short and fun—no longer than 10 to 15 minutes. Dogs have short attention spans and you will notice that after about 15 minutes their performance will begin to suffer unless a lot of play is involved. To continue to train a tired or bored dog will result in the training of bad habits, resentment in the dog, and frustration for the trainer. Especially when training a young puppy, or when you only have one or two different exercises to practice, quit while you are ahead! Keep your greyhound wanting more, and you will have a happy, willing, obedience partner.

Not by the book: Finally, nothing will ever go just as perfectly as it seems to in all of the training instructions. But although there may be setbacks, you can train your dog, as long as you remember to be consistent, firm, gentle, realistic, and most of all, patient.

Dress for Success

Equipment for training should include a six-foot (2 m) web or leather lead and a 20-foot (6 m) lightweight lead. Most greyhounds can be trained with a buckle collar, but a choke collar is also an acceptable choice as long as you know how to use it correctly. A choke collar is not for choking! The proper way to administer a correction with a choke collar is with a gentle snap, then immediate release. If you think of the point of the correction as being to startle the dog by the sound of the chain links moving, rather than to choke your dog, you will be correcting with the

81

HOW-TO:
Solving Behavior Problems

Punishment won't help. Dogs do not destroy items when you leave out of spite, but more often, anxiety. Put the dog in another room until you calm down and plan to begin training to thwart its separation anxiety.

Even greyhounds misbehave—but usually not on purpose. Many of these problems can be avoided or cured.

Digging and chewing: One of the joys of greyhound ownership is that you will always come home to a exuberant reunion. But that reunion will be far less joyous if you open your front door to what appears to be a nuclear test site.

Adult dogs may dig or destroy items through curiosity or boredom. The best way to deal with these dogs is to provide daily physical and mental interaction, especially an hour or so before leaving the house, tiring both the greyhound's body and mind. If this doesn't work, and especially if matters go from bad to worse, you more likely have a case of separation anxiety on your hands.

Separation anxiety is probably the single most misunderstood and common dog behavior problem of urban dogs. Even the most well-behaved greyhound may mangle its owner's home and possessions when left alone.

But an observant owner will notice some things that are different about the dog that destroys only when left alone. For one, the dog often appears to be highly agitated when the owner returns. For another, the sites of destruction are often around doors, windows, or fences, suggestive of an attempt to escape. Such dogs

are reacting to the anxiety of being left alone, an intensely stressful situation for a social animal. But the average owner, upon returning home to such ruin, punishes the dog. This in no way alleviates the anxiety of being left alone; it does, however, eventually create anxiety associated with the owner's return home, and this in turn tends to escalate the destructive behavior.

Instead the dog must be conditioned to overcome its fear of separation. This is done by separating the dog for very short periods of time and gradually working to longer periods, taking care never to allow the dog to become anxious during any session. This is complicated when you must leave your dog for long periods during the conditioning program. In these cases the part of the house or yard in which the dog is left for long periods should be different from the part in which the conditioning sessions take place; the latter location should be the location in which you wish to leave the dog after conditioning is completed.

In either case, when you return home, no matter how

your house looks, greet your dog calmly or even ignore it for a few minutes, to emphasize the point that being left was really no big deal. Then have the dog perform a simple trick or obedience exercise so that you have an excuse to praise it. Separation anxiety is a problem that should be cured, not sidestepped. Drug therapy may be necessary in severe cases.

House soiling: When a dog soils the house, the first question to be asked is was the dog ever really completely housebroken? If the answer is no, you must begin housebreaking anew. Sometimes a housebroken dog will be forced to soil the house because of a bout of diarrhea, and afterwards will continue to soil in the same area. If this happens, restrict the dog from that area, and revert to basic housebreaking lessons once again. Submissive dogs may urinate upon greeting you; punishment only makes this worse. Keep greetings calm, don't bend over or otherwise dominate the dog, and usually this can be outgrown. Some dogs defecate or urinate because of the stress of separation anxiety; you must treat the anxiety to cure the symptom. Older dogs may simply not have the bladder control that they had as youngsters; paper training or a doggy door is the best solution for them. Older spayed females may "dribble"; ask your veterinarian about estrogen supplementation that may help. Younger dogs may have lost control due to an infection; several small urine spots are a sign that a trip to the veterinarian is needed. Male dogs may "lift their leg" inside the house as a means of marking it as theirs. Castration will usually solve this problem; otherwise diligent deodorizing and the use of some dog-deterring odorants (available at pet stores) may help.

Fearfulness: Ex-racing greyhounds are remarkably well-adjusted considering that their former world was so different from the home life you are now offering them. However, your greyhound should never be pushed into situations that might overwhelm it. A program of gradual desensitization, with the dog exposed to the frightening person or thing and then rewarded for calm behavior, is time-consuming but the best way to alleviate any fear. Strangers should be asked to ignore shy dogs. Dogs seem to fear the attention of a stranger more than they fear the strangers themselves.

Never coddle your dog when it acts afraid, because it reinforces the behavior. It is always useful if your greyhound knows a few simple commands; performing these exercises correctly gives you a reason to praise the dog and also increases the dog's sense of security because it knows what is expected of it.

Aggression: Greyhounds are about as mild-mannered as a dog can be. A greyhound that is aggressive toward a human is a rare but dangerous individual, and it is unlikely that such a greyhound would ever be made available for adoption or sale. There are several reasons for biting, with one of the more common in greyhounds being fear. The best treatment is to go through a careful fear-desensitizing program as outlined previously. Avoid staring into the eyes of any greyhound with a tendency to bite. Staring a dog directly in the eye is interpreted by the dog as a threat.

If you don't know why your greyhound is acting aggressively, schedule an appointment with your veterinarian to discuss possible physiological problems, such as hypothyroidism. An old dog may suddenly bite because it is arthritic and in pain. Many such problems can be treated with drug therapy.

If you worry that your greyhound may bite before you can effect a cure, remember that track greyhounds are used to wearing muzzles. Order a kennel muzzle from the NGA and have your greyhound wear it in delicate situations.

More common is aggressive behavior toward other animals, specifically cats. A greyhound cannot be expected, without specific training, to read your mind and cuddle with kitty (see page 32). Having your greyhound perform a few simple obedience exercises with the cat present can help focus its attention on you and give you an excuse to reward it.

However, don't take a chance with your neighbor's beloved pets or with your greyhound's own safety. When outside of your yard, keep it on a leash.

Aggression toward other dogs is rare. On occasion two dogs that live together may be vying for dominance, and fights will occur until one dog emerges as the clear victor. But even in cases where one dog is dominant, fights may erupt when both are competing for the owner's attention. The dominant dog expects to get that attention before the subordinate. This is one case where playing favorites (to the dominant dog) will actually be a favor to the subordinate dog in the long run!

Barking: Barking is seldom a problem in greyhounds. Isolated dogs might bark as a means of getting attention and alleviating loneliness, even if that attention includes punishment. The simplest solution is to move the dog's domain to a less isolated location. The dog that must spend the day home alone is a greater challenge. Again, the simplest solution is to change the situation, perhaps by adding another animal—a good excuse to get two greyhounds!

Jumping up: Greyhounds think nothing of wrapping their legs around their owner's shoulders to greet them face to face, but this can be an annoying and dangerous trick. The simplest solution is to simply step backwards so your dog's feet meet only air. Kneel down to praise and greet the dog on its level.

Awaiting its handler's next command during an obedience trial, a greyhound shows the rapt attention that comes from learning the "watch me" command.

training session; there are too many tragic cases where a choke collar really did earn its name after being snagged on a fence, bush, or even a dog play-mate's tooth.

What Every Good Greyhound Should Know

Sit: There is a myth even among greyhound owners that greyhounds cannot sit. It is true that greyhounds are not a breed that naturally spends time sitting, but they are quite capable of sitting and they can remain sitting for the one to three minutes needed to pass an obedience trial.

With your greyhound (named "Hypatia"), say "Hypatia, sit", and gently push up and slightly back with your left hand under her chin. You can also use your right arm to push (not karate chop!) forward behind her "knees." You are, in essence, folding your greyhound into position. Once she is in position, praise lavishly. With a chowhound, you can try holding a tidbit a bit above and behind your greyhound's head, at the same time pressing gently on its hindquarters. Then praise and give it its just reward.

Don't try to push down your greyhound's rear in order to achieve a sit. The greyhound will simply push against you, and you will more likely just teach your dog to tense its rear rather than sit.

"Watch Me": A common problem when training any dog is that the dog's attention is elsewhere. You can teach your dog to pay attention to you by teaching it the "watch me" command. With your greyhound sitting, say "watch me," and when it looks in your direction, give it a treat or other reward. Gradually require the dog to look at you for longer and longer periods before rewarding it. Teach "watch me" before going on to the other commands.

Stay: Next comes the Stay command. Tell your greyhound to "Sit,"

right level of force, and won't risk hurting your greyhound's sensitive neck. The choke collar is placed on the dog so that the ring with the lead attached comes up around the left side of the dog's neck, and through the other ring. If put on backwards, it will not release itself after being tightened (since you will be on the right side of your dog for most training). The choke collar should never be left on your greyhound after a praise her, then say "Stay" in a soothing voice (you do not have to precede the Stay command with the dog's name, because you should already have the dog's attention). Start with simply requiring her to stay in the sit position beside you for up to 30 seconds. Then praise and give a release command ("OK!"). If your greyhound attempts to get up or lie down, gently place her back into position. After the dog is staying reliably, command "Stay," step out (starting with your right foot) and turn to stand directly in front of her. If your dog tries to come to you, just place her back in position and repeat "Stay." Work up to longer times, and then back away and repeat the process. Eventually you should be able to walk confidently away longer and longer distances, and for longer and longer times. The point is not to push your dog to the limit, but to let it succeed. To do this you must be very patient, and you must increase your times and distances in very small increments. Always return when the dog is still staying so that you can praise. Don't make the mistake of staring intently at the dog during the Stay, because this is perceived by the dog as a threat and often intimidates it so that it squirms out of position.

Come: When both "Sit" and "Stay" are mastered, you are ready to introduce "Come." Never have your dog come to you and then scold it for something it has done. In the dog's mind it is being scolded for coming, not for any earlier misdeed.

To teach the command "Come," have your greyhound sit, and with leash attached, command "Stay" and step out to the end of the leash and face your dog. This Stay will be a little different for your dog, as you will drop to your knees, open your arms, and invite her with an enthusiastic "Hypatia, Come!" An unsure dog can be coaxed with a tug on the lead or

An obedience trained greyhound is a pleasure at home, in public, and in the wilds.

the sight of a tidbit. Remember to really praise; after all, you have enticed her to break the Stay command, and she may be uneasy about that. During the training for Come, it is not unusual for there to be some regression in the performance of "Stay" due to confusion; just be gentle, patient, and consistent and this will sort itself out.

The next step is to again place the dog in the Sit/Stay, walk to the end of the lead, call "Hypatia, Come," and quickly back away several steps, coaxing the dog to you. Eventually you can go to your longer leash, and walk quickly backwards as far as your equilibrium will allow. This encourages the dog to come at a brisk pace; in fact

Dogs are more inclined to come if you get down to their level. Always make the come command fun and exciting for your dog.

most dogs will regard this as an especially fun game! Of course, in real life the dog is seldom sitting when you want it to come, so once it understands what you mean by come, allow your dog to walk on lead, and at irregular intervals call "Hypatia, Come," run backwards, and when she reaches you be sure to praise. Finally, attach a longer line, allow her to meander about, and in the midst of her investigations, call, walk backwards, and praise.

"Come" is the most important command your greyhound will ever learn. You will eventually want to practice it in the presence of distractions, such as other leashed dogs, unfamiliar people, cats, and cars. Always practice on lead. If it takes a tidbit as a reward to get your greyhound motivated, then this is an instance where you should use an occasional food reward. Coming on command is more than a cute trick; it could save your greyhound's life.

Down: When you need your greyhound to stay in one place for any long periods of time it is best for it to be left in a Down/Stay. Begin teaching the Down command with the dog in the sitting position. If you are using food rewards, command "Hypatia, Down,"

then show her a tidbit and move it below her nose toward the ground. If she reaches down to get it, give it to her. Repeat, requiring her to reach farther down (without lifting her rear from the ground) until she has to lower her elbows to the ground. You can help her here by reaching under her and easing her front legs out in front of her.

If you do not wish to use food rewards, again start with the dog sitting on your left, command "Hypatia, Down," then place your left hand on her withers (right over her shoulders) and with your right hand gently grasp both front legs and ease her to the ground. Never try to cram your dog into the down position, which could not only cause injuries (to you!), but scare a submissive dog and cause many dogs to resist.

Practice the Down/Stay just as you did the Sit/Stay. In fact your dog now has quite a repertoire of behaviors that you can combine in different ways to combat boredom. The only thing left for any well-behaved greyhound is the ability to walk politely on lead.

Heel: Most track dogs already know how to walk politely on lead, put some may still need some lessons. If you have a puppy, the first step is to introduce it to the leash, using the lightweight show-type lead. If you have followed this training sequence, your pup should already be acquainted with the leash at least by the time it has learned "Come." Still, walking alongside of you on lead is a new experience for a young baby, and many will freeze in their tracks once they discover their freedom is being violated. In this case do not simply drag the pup along, but coax it with praise, and if need be, food, until it's walking somewhere, anywhere. When the puppy follows you, praise and reward. In this way the pup comes to realize that following you while walking on lead pays off.

The correct heel position is with the dog on your left side with its neck next to and parallel with your leg. Say "Hypatia, Heel" and step off with your left foot first. (Remember that you stepped off on your right foot when you left your dog on a Stay; if you are consistent, the leg that moves first will provide an eye-level cue for your dog.) During your first few practice sessions you will keep her on a short lead, holding her in heel position, and of course praising her. When you stop, have her sit. While some trainers advocate letting the dog lunge to the end of the lead and then snapping it back, such an approach is unfair if you haven't shown the dog what is expected of it at first, and such methods are not appropriate for a greyhound. Instead, after a few sessions of showing the dog the heel position, give her a little more loose lead; if she stays in heel position, praise; more likely she will not, in which case pull her back to position with a quick gentle snap, then release, of the lead. If, after a few days practice, your dog still seems oblivious to your efforts, turn unexpectedly several times; teach your dog that it is its responsibility to keep an eye on you.

Keep up a good pace; too slow a pace gives dogs time to sniff, to look all around and in general become distracted; a brisk pace will focus the dog's attention upon you and generally aid training. As you progress you will want to add some right turns, left turns, and about-faces, and walk at all different speeds. Then practice in different areas (still always on lead) and around different distractions. Vary your routine to combat boredom, and keep training sessions short. Adult dogs should be taught that heeling is not the time to relieve themselves (if you give them the chance to relieve themselves before the training session, and then keep up a brisk pace, they will seldom have the "urge").

To teach a greyhound to lie down on command, ease its legs forward when it is sitting. Keep your other hand on its back to prevent it from getting up. Never use a leash to pull your dog down to the ground.

Higher Education

Is your greyhound "gifted"? Perhaps you would like to take it to obedience classes, where both of you can learn even more, practice around distractions, and discuss problems with people who have similar interests. Most cities have obedience clubs that conduct classes. The AKC or your local Humane Society can direct you to them. You might also contact the Greyhound Club of America or a greyhound adoption agency and ask for names of greyhound obedience enthusiasts in your area. Attend a local obedience trial (contact the AKC for date and location) and ask local owners of happy working dogs (especially greyhounds) where they train. Be forewarned that a greyhound is not a retriever; don't expect it to wag its tail in glee for no apparent reason while it goes through its paces. This doesn't mean that the greyhound doesn't enjoy obedience; it just has a more subtle way of showing it. Not all instructors may understand the greyhound

Even though a greyhound may not wag its tail when it is put through its paces in obedience classes, its expression reveals the pleasure it derives from a job well done.

psyche, and not all classes may be right for you and your greyhound.

You may wish to enter an obedience trial yourself eventually, in which case the advice of fellow competitors will be invaluable. Obedience competitors love their sport; they love to welcome newcomers, and they love to see them succeed; most of all they love their dogs and understand how you love yours. Greyhounds are adept, if different, obedience pupils, and you and your dog could very well become a successful team.

Fun with Greyhounds

Mind Games

The problem with useful commands like Sit and Stay is that they don't exactly astound your friends. For that you need something flashy, some incredible feat of intelligence and dexterity: a dog trick. Greyhounds aren't the standard trick dog, but they can easily manage to jump a stick. Start with the stick low to the ground, perhaps resting atop of two blocks. Command "Jump," step over the stick with your greyhound, and gradually increase the height. Once your greyhound knows the command, then stand beside the stick and repeat the procedure. Finally, hold the stick. Once the stick is mastered, you can try a hoop, starting once again at ground zero. Greyhounds love to jump, and this will quickly become their favorite trick!

Another easily taught trick is "shake hands." With your dog sitting, command "Shake," and then gently push your dog to the side just enough so that it must lift up one foot for balance. Reward with a treat and gradually require the paw to be lifted higher. Some dogs will go so far as to paw at your hand holding the treat, which makes further teaching very simple. "Shake" is a good icebreaker for therapy dogs (see page 98) or for dogs that spend time with children.

Lure-coursing is one of many fun greyhound activities.

One of the greyhound's favorite and most impressive tricks is jumping a stick.

Obedience Trials

You plan on training your greyhound the commands Heel, Sit, Down, Come, and Stay for use in everyday life. Add the "stand for exam" (which most track greyhounds already generally know), and your dog will have the basic skills necessary to earn the AKC Companion Dog (CD) title. The hard part is doing it amidst the frenzied barking of a dog show; that is, the hard part for most dogs. But for the ex-racer, a mere thousand dogs is nothing compared to several thousand screaming fans. Another greyhound unfair advantage! The AKC will send you a free pamphlet describing obedience trial regulations, and you will need to get an ILP or AKC number in order to enter a trial (see page 75).

Specifically, the AKC CD title requires the dog to do the following:
1. Heel on lead, sitting automatically each time you stop, negotiating right, left, and about turns without guidance from you, and changing to a faster and slower pace.
2. Heel in a figure 8 around two people, still on lead.

3. Stand still off lead six feet (2 m) away from you and allow a judge to touch its body.
4. Do the exercises in number 1, except off lead.
5. Come to you when called from 20 feet (6 m) away, and then return to heel position on command.
6. Stay for one minute in a sitting position with a group of other dogs, while you are 20 feet (6 m) away.
7. Stay for three minutes in a down position with the same group while you are 20 feet (6 m) away.

Each exercise has points assigned to it, and points are deducted for the inevitable imperfections. In all but the heel commands, you may give a command only one time, and in no cases may you touch, speak to, physically guide, correct, praise, or do anything except give the dog's name, followed by the command during that exercise. No food can be carried into the ring. The dog must pass each individual exercise to qualify, and to earn the degree it must qualify three times.

Higher degrees of Companion Dog Excellent (CDX) or Utility Dog (UD) and Utility Dog Excellent (UDX) also require retrieving, jumping, hand signals, and scent discrimination. Although greyhounds aren't known for their retrieving or scenting prowess, they have nonetheless handily obtained CDX and UD titles. In fact, they seem to enjoy these higher level exercises more than the elementary lessons. The OTCH degree is an Obedience Trial Champion; these are given only to dogs with UDs that outscore many other UD dogs in many, many trials. If you are at an obedience trial and see that an OTCH dog of any breed is entered, take the time to watch it go through its paces. As of yet there is no OTCH greyhound. Could yours be the first?

If you enter competition with your greyhound, remember this as your golden rule: Companion Dog means just that; being upset at your dog because it messed up defeats the purpose of obedience as a way of promoting a harmonious partnership between trainer and dog. Failing a trial, in the perspective of life, is an insignificant event. Never let a ribbon or a few points become more important than a trusting relationship with your companion. Besides, your greyhound will forgive you for the times you mess up!

The Greyhound Good Citizen

In formal recognition of dogs that behave in public, the AKC offers the Canine Good Citizen (CGC) certificate. To earn this title your greyhound must pass the following exercises:

• Accepting the greeting of a friendly stranger.
• Sitting politely for petting by a stranger.
• Allowing a stranger to pet and groom it.
• Walking politely on a loose lead.
• Walking through a crowd on a lead.
• Sitting and lying down on command and staying in place while on a 20-foot (6 m) line.
• Calming down after play.
• Reacting politely to another dog.
• Reacting calmly to distractions.
• Remaining calm when tied for three minutes in the owner's absence, under supervision by a stranger.

The CGC is perhaps the most important title your greyhound can earn. The most magnificent champion in the show or obedience ring is no credit to its breed if it is not a good public citizen in the real world.

Tracking

Hot on the trail, the hound lunges against its harness, eagerly following a scent laid some hours before. A bloodhound, perhaps? No, a greyhound! For a dog that is supposed to be a sighthound, greyhounds do a good scenthound imitation. Several greyhounds have earned the tough Tracking Dog (TD) and even tougher Tracking Dog Excellent (TDX) titles, requiring them to follow a trail by scent. The road to a tracking title is a lonely and long one; but what better companion to have on such a venture than a greyhound?

You can evaluate your greyhound's propensity to use its nose by hiding dog biscuits around the house or yard and then having your greyhound sniff them out. This is the basis for one popular method of training: treats are dropped every few feet along a trail laid by the owner (or other tracklayer), and the dog is encouraged to find them. The dog gradually learns that by following the trail it will come across hidden treasures. Eventually fewer and fewer treats are used, but there is the mother lode of dog biscuits awaiting at the end of the trail. Tracking aficionados are perhaps the most devoted of dog trainers, and enjoy the solitude of spending the morning alone with their special dog. Best of all, the dogs love it!

Search and Rescue: Have you ever dreamed of being a hero? You and your greyhound could be somebody's hero because dogs trained in search and rescue use their noses (and other senses) to find lost people or bodies. The ever ready and versatile greyhound has already proven itself in this endeavor as well, though their numbers are still extremely limited.

Agility

Greyhounds define agility. But competitive agility challenges dogs to run, jump, balance, weave, freeze, and tunnel, all off lead. Obstacles include an A-frame, seesaw, elevated boardwalk, tunnels, and a variety of high and broad jumps (adjusted according to the height of the dog). There are Novice, Open, and Excellent classes, and the AKC awards, in increasing level of

Plenty of fun can be had in your own backyard.

A greyhound warms up on an A-frame prior to an agility competition.

difficulty, the titles Novice Agility Dog (NAD), Open Agility Dog (OAD), Agility Dog Excellent (ADE), and Master Agility Excellent (MAX). No greyhound has yet earned an agility title, but several are in hot pursuit.

Since agility competition is a comparatively new sport, you may have difficulty finding a group with which to train, but you can practice some of the elements on your own. Playgrounds or your own living room can be used as practice arenas. Some resourceful trainers have used a dozen plumber's helpers as weaving poles (ignoring the questioning looks of the people watching them buy them!) or a line of chairs with a sheet draped over them as a tunnel.

Even more competitive fun with greyhounds can be had in showing or coursing, described elsewhere in this book. But no one can deny that the very most fun with greyhounds comes with snuggling on a cold evening, sharing a sunrise, or collapsing after a good game of tag—and luckily, no one has yet devised a competition for them.

The Show Greyhound

"A Grehound shold be heeded lyke a snake

And neckyd lyke a drake,
Backed lyke a beam,
Syded lyke a bream,
Footed lyke a catte,
Taylled lyke a ratte."

—Dame Juliana Berners, Abbess of Sopewell, 1486

So, in Middle English, read the earliest version of the greyhound standard, the blueprint of the ideal greyhound. From head to tail, it describes those attributes that make a greyhound look like a greyhound. This possession of breed attributes is known as type, and has been an important requirement of any greyhound then and now. A dog should also be built in such a way that it can go about its daily life with minimal exertion and absence of lameness. This equally important attribute is known as soundness. Add to these the attributes of good health and temperament, and you have the four cornerstones of the ideal greyhound.

The AKC Greyhound Standard

Head—Long and narrow, fairly wide between the ears, scarcely perceptible stop, little or no development of nasal sinuses, good length of muzzle, which

The greyhound is a blend of grace, litheness, and power, exemplified by this top winning open field courser, the product of generations of selective breeding for both field and show capabilities from a combination of AKC and NGA ancestors.

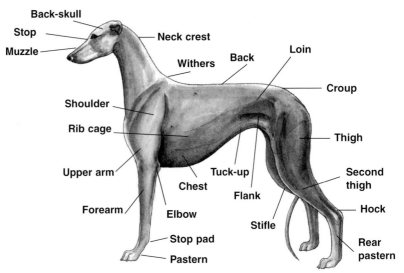

The external parts of the greyhound.

should be powerful without coarseness. Teeth very strong and even in front.

Ears—Small and fine in texture, thrown back and folded, except when excited, when they are semipricked.

Eyes—Dark, bright, intelligent, indicating spirit.

Neck—Long, muscular, without throatiness, slightly arched and widening gradually into the shoulder.

Shoulders—Placed as obliquely as possible, muscular without being loaded.

Forelegs— Perfectly straight, set well into the shoulders, neither turned in nor out, pasterns strong.

Chest—Deep, and as wide as consistent with speed, fairly well-sprung ribs.

Back—Muscular and broad.

Loins—Good depth of muscle, well-arched, well cut-up in the flanks.

Hindquarters—Long, very muscular and powerful, wide and well-let-down, well-bent stifles. Hocks well-bent and rather close to ground, wide but straight fore and aft.

Feet—Hard and close, rather more hare- than cat-feet, well-knuckled up with good strong claws.

Tail—Long, fine, and tapering with a slight upward curve.

Coat—Short, smooth, and firm in texture.

Color—Immaterial.

Weight—Dogs, 65 to 70 pounds; bitches, 60 to 65 pounds.

Standard Terms:
- stop: the transition from backskull to muzzle
- throatiness: flab around the throat
- loaded shoulders: overly muscled shoulders
- well-let-down: near to the ground
- hare foot: long narrow foot
- cat foot: round foot

Scale of Points

General symmetry and quality	10
Head and neck	20
Chest and shoulders	20
Back	10
Quarters	20
Legs and feet	20
Total	100

What Color Is Your Greyhound?

One of the wonderful things about greyhounds is the rainbow of colors and patterns available. The American Greyhound Track Operators publishes a chart of the possible colors, but many greyhounders find it interesting to take an analytical approach to describing greyhound colors and the genes that control them, as follows:

White: In greyhounds, there are four different alleles (alternate forms of a gene for one trait) for different degrees of white spotting, with more white always recessive to less white. In decreasing order of dominance, the alleles of the S gene are:

S: "self-colored," dogs with no white. All such dogs must have at least one copy of S. But because S could mask any of the more recessive alleles, such dogs could be either S/S, S/s^i, S/s^p, or S/s^w.

s^i: next in dominance, s^i causes the so-called "irish-marked" pattern: white feet (and perhaps legs), tail tip, and collar. Such dogs could not have S, but could have one of three allele combinations: either s^i/s^i, s^i/s^p, or s^i/s^w.

s^p: "parti-color": predominantly white with patches of color. Such dogs can either be s^p/s^p or s^p/s^w.

s^w: mostly white, with a very few or no small patches of color. Because this is the most recessive allele, such dogs would need two copies of it: s^w/s^w.

A separate gene controls whether or not there are lots of tiny spots (so called ticking) on otherwise white areas. The allele for ticking (T) is dominant to the allele for no ticking (t).

Black: You can think of the white areas on your greyhound as though a bucket of paint had been splashed over the dog, partially obscuring its "true" color beneath. Look beyond any white and see if you notice any pattern of black hair distribution. Black distribution is controlled by several alleles at

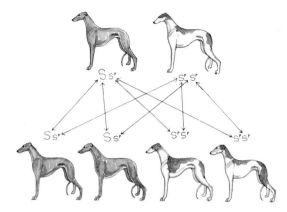

If a solid colored dog carrying a recessive gene for spotting is bred to a spotted dog, on average half of the offspring will be solid colored and half will be spotted.

two different gene locations, A and E, which sometimes interact.

A: dominant, results in a pure black dog. Genotype could be A/A or A/a^y.

a^y: produces a tan or red color. They have the genotype of a^y/a^y.

The E series is more complicated.

E^m: results in a black muzzle (which would not be visible on a black dog).

E: next in dominance, this results in a solid color without a black muzzle.

e^{br}: results in brindle: irregular vertical black stripes running down the sides of the body over a lighter background.

e: dogs with e will have no black hair anywhere, even if they are A/A. In a manner of speaking, it "overrides" the A gene.

Thus red greyhounds are a^y/a^y E/- or a^y/a^y E^m/- (where the "-" denotes either E^m, E, e^{br}, or e), and fawn greyhounds are A/A ee or A/a^{y}ee.

Saturation: The D gene controls whether colors are diluted:

D: dominant; allows intense, fully saturated colors.

d: recessive; makes all colors less saturated, and especially makes

The curvaceous smooth lines of the show greyhound define elegance.

blacks more gray (or "blue"). Eye color also tends to be lighter.

The C gene also controls dilution of colors:

C: dominant; allows intense, fully saturated colors.

These show beauties exemplify the sweet yet keen expression so typical of the greyhound.

c^{ch}: recessive; decreases the red or tan coloration while allowing black to remain fully dark black, although its effect is also modified by other genes.

Color is immaterial in either the show ring, the race track, or your heart, but it is an integral part of the special beauty that defines every individual greyhound.

Showing a Greyhound

Conformation shows evaluate your greyhound on the basis of the official breed standard. A judge will examine each dog from the tip of its nose to the tip of its tail, feeling its body structure, studying its way of moving, and looking at the total picture it creates. If you have gone out of your way to get a show-quality greyhound, chances are you will want to show it. Most people don't get an ex-racing dog with the idea of showing it, but it, too, can be shown if it has not already been neutered and if you can obtain an AKC registration (not ILP) number (see page 17).

Greyhounds are a very easy breed to show. There is no fancy grooming and no spiffy showmanship required. But even the best dog needs a little work before showing off. Practice posing your greyhound with all four feet pointing forward, legs parallel to each other and perpendicular to the ground, and head held high. Your greyhound should also know how to trot proudly in a dead straight line on a loose show lead (a very thin leash). The most common mistake new handlers make is to demand that their dogs stand like statues for so long that the poor dogs become bored, and then they wonder why the dog hates to show. A happy attitude will overshadow a myriad of faults. Professional handlers can show your dog for you and probably win more often than you would; however, there is nothing like the thrill of winning when you are on the other end of the lead!

Contact your local kennel or even obedience club and find out if they have handling classes, or when the next match will be held. Matches are informal events where everybody learns: puppies, handlers, even the judges. Win or lose, never take one judge's opinion too seriously, and no matter how obviously feebleminded the judge is, be polite and keep your comments to yourself.

Grooming for the show ring begins long before the show. Long thick winter coats need to go. Use a shedding blade or rubber brush to remove dead hair. Dandruff-prone dogs are best washed a few days (rather than immediately) before the show. A mink oil spray rubbed in on the day of the show can help the coat shine. Cut any straggler hairs, and neaten the hair along the tuck-up and under the tail. Many people cut the vibrissae (whiskers) for a neater and more professional appearance, but leaving these important sensory organs intact is becoming more fashionable.

You, too, must be groomed; you don't want to embarrass your greyhound. For shows proper attire is a sports jacket for men, skirt with flat shoes for women; at matches the dress code is less formal.

At a real AKC show, each time a judge chooses your dog as the best dog of its sex that is not already a Champion it wins up to 5 points, depending upon how many dogs it defeats. Unfortunately, in many parts of the country you may have difficulty finding enough competition. To become an AKC Champion (CH) your greyhound must win 15 points, including two majors (defeating enough dogs to win 3 to 5 points at a time). You may enter any class for which your dog is eligible: Puppy, Novice, American Bred, Bred by Exhibitor, or Open. The Best of Breed class is for dogs that are already Champions. If you are lucky enough to win Best of Breed, be sure to stick around to compete in the hound group

Two shades of brindles engage in a lazy dog's game of mouth wrestling.

later in the day. The winner of the hound group then competes with the winner of the other six groups for the Best in Show award. Greyhounds have been extremely competitive show dogs throughout the years, but none so much as the incomparable CH Aroi Talk of the Blues, who won over 68 Best in Shows and was the top show dog of all breeds in 1976.

Before entering you should contact the AKC and ask for the rules and regulations concerning dog shows, which will explain the requirements for each class. Your dog must be entered about three weeks before the show date, and you will need to get a premium list and entry form from the appropriate show superintendent (addresses are available from the AKC or most dog magazines).

To survive as a conformation competitor you must be able to separate your own ego and self-esteem from your dog; many people cannot do this. You must also not allow your dog's ability to win in the ring cloud your perception of your dog's true worth in its primary role: that of friend and companion. Your greyhound never has to step foot in a show ring, win a race, earn a title, or thrill anyone except you to be first place in your heart.

The Greyhound Companion

Living with a greyhound means having a friend who is never (well, seldom) critical or judgmental, who always greets you with glee, who is always willing to cuddle on lonely evenings, and frolic on sunny afternoons. A greyhound will make you get out of the house, and once out, is a magnet for meeting people. Greyhounds bring joy to life; have you ever thought of sharing that joy?

Sharing your Greyhound

Studies have shown that pet ownership increases life expectancy and that petting animals can lower blood pressure. But at a certain point in life many older people can no longer keep a pet, often because they live in nursing homes where pets are not allowed to live. But most nursing homes allow pets to visit. And if you ever see how a visit from a dog can light up the faces

The calm and gentle-natured greyhound is a natural for visiting the elderly.

and lives of those lonely people who may have relied upon the companionship of a pet throughout most of their independent years, then you will be back again and again. A greyhound, with its calm demeanor, lustrous eyes, soft ears, and dramatic appearance, is a natural. Dogs can be registered as Certified Therapy Dogs by demonstrating that they act in an obedient, outgoing, gentle manner to strangers. Your greyhound could make a difference.

For Better or Worse

Even if you can't share your greyhound with others, you will be sharing your life with your pet. Both of you will change through the years. Be sure that you remember the promise you made to yourself and your future greyhound before you made the commitment to share your life: to keep your interest in your dog and care for it every day of its life with as much love and enthusiasm as you did the first day it arrived home. But if you find that things are not working out, contact a greyhound adoption center and ask for guidance.

Till Death Do Us Part

The greyhound that finds a loving and permanent home is a lucky dog indeed. And so is the human half of the partnership. But there comes the time when, no matter how diligent you have been, neither you nor your veterinarian can prevent your greyhound from succumbing to old age or an incurable illness. It seems hard to believe that you will have to say goodbye to one who has been such a focal point of your life—in truth, a real member of your family. That dogs live such a short time compared to humans is a cruel fact, and as much as you may wish otherwise, your greyhound is a dog and is not immortal.

You should realize that both of you have been fortunate to have shared so many good times, but make sure that your greyhound's remaining time is still pleasurable, or at least, comfortable. Many terminal illnesses make your dog feel very bad, and there comes a point where your desire to keep your friend with you as long as possible may not be the kindest thing for either of you. Ask your vet if there is a reasonable chance of your dog's getting better, and if it is likely your dog is suffering. Ask yourself if your dog is getting pleasure out of life, and if it enjoys most of its days. If your greyhound no longer eats its dinner or treats, this is a sign that it does not feel well and you must face the prospect of doing what is best for your beloved friend. Euthanasia is painless and involves giving an overdose of an anesthetic. If your dog is scared of the clinic, you might feel better having the doctor meet you at home or come out to your car. Although it won't be easy, try to remain with your greyhound so that its last moments will be filled with your love; otherwise enlist a friend that your dog knows to stay with your dog. Try to recall the wonderful times you have shared and realize that however painful it is to lose such a once-in-a-lifetime dog, it is better than never having had such a friend in the first place.

Many people who regarded their pet as a member of the family nonetheless feel embarrassed at the grief they feel at its loss. Yet this dog has often functioned as a surrogate child, best friend, and confidant. We should all be lucky enough to find a human with the faithful and loving qualities of our dogs. In some ways the loss of a pet can be harder than that of more distant family members, especially because the support from friends that comes with human loss is too often absent with pet loss. Such well-meaning but ill-informed statements as "he was just a dog" or "just get another one" do little to ease the pain, but the truth is that many people simply don't know how to react and probably aren't really as callous as they might sound. There are, however, many people who share your feelings and there are pet bereavement counselors available at many veterinary schools.

After losing such a dog, many people say they will never get another. True, no dog will ever take the place of your dog. But you will find that another dog is a welcome diversion and will help keep you from dwelling on the loss of your first pet, as long as you don't keep comparing the new dog to the old. True also, by getting another dog you are sentencing yourself to the same grief in another ten years or so, but wouldn't you rather have that than miss out on all of the love and companionship altogether? Besides, somewhere out there is a greyhound with soulful eyes and a big heart—a greyhound waiting for you.

An ex-racer soaks up the good life—both it and its owner are lucky to have found each other.

Somewhere out there a greyhound is waiting for you; a 40 mph couch potato with a big heart.

Useful Addresses and Literature

Organizations

American Kennel Club
51 Madison Ave.
New York, NY 10038
(212) 696-8200

AKC Registration and
  Information
5580 Centerview Drive, Ste 200
Raleigh, NC 27606-3390
(919) 233-9767

Greyhound Club of America
  (AKC)*
Ms. Marsha Wartell, Secretary
3433 Cartagena
Corpus Christi, TX 78418

National Greyhound Association
P.O. Box 543
Abilene, KS 67410
(913) 263-4660

American Sighthound Field
  Association
C/O P.O. Box 399
Alpaugh, CA 93201

The Greyhound Project, Inc.
261 Robbins St.
Milton, MA 02186

Greyhound Protection League
(415) 327-0631

*Note: The above address will
change with the election of new club
officers. Contact the AKC for the
current listing.

Greyhound Pets of America
1-800-366-1472
(your call will be routed to the
nearest adoption chapter)

American Boarding Kennel
  Association
4575 Galley Road, Suite 400A
Colorado Springs, CO 80915

Orthopedic Foundation for
  Animals
2300 Nifong Boulevard
Colombia, MO 65201
(314) 442-0418

Home Again Microchip System
1-800-LONELY ONE

Magazines

Dog World
29 North Wacker Drive
Chicago, IL 60606-3298
(312) 726-2802

Dog Fancy
P.O. Box 53264
Boulder, CO 80322-3264
(303) 666-8504

The greyhound is more of a partner and soulmate than a pet.

Dogs USA Annual
P.O. Box 55811
Boulder, CO 80322-5811
(303) 786-7652

The Sighthound Review
(AKC oriented)
P.O. Box 30430
Santa Barbara, CA 93130
(805) 966-7270

The Greyhound Review
Official publication of the NGA
See NGA address under
    Organizations

AKC Gazette
Official publication of the AKC
See AKC New York address
    under Organizations

Field Advisory News
Official publication of ASFA
See ASFA address under
    Organizations

Books

Ash, Edward C. *The Book of
the Greyhound.* Hutchinson &
Co., London. 1933.

Barnes, Julia. *The Complete
Book of Greyhounds.* Howell.
1994.

Blythe, Linda L., Gannon,
James R., & Craig, A. Morrie.
*Care of the Racing
Greyhound: A Guide for
Trainers, Breeders, and
Veterinarians.* American
Greyhound Council. 1994.
(Good medical text; available
from the NGA).

Branigan, Cynthia. *Adopting the
Racing Greyhound.* Howell,
1992.

Burnham, Patricia G.
Playtraining Your Dog.
St.Martin Press, 1980. (A
whole book about obedience
training greyhounds!)

Edwards, Clark H. *The
Greyhound.* Popular Dogs
Publishing Co Ltd., London,
England. 1973.

Gaines *Touring With Towser*
P.O. Box 8172
Kankakee, IL 60901
(lists motels that accept pets)

Hutchinson, William. *Hutchinson
on Sighthounds.* (Reprint of
the sighthound sections
of *Hutchinson's Dog
Encyclopedia*, originally
published 1934). Hoflin
Publishing, Wheat Ridge, CO.
1976. (History of all
sighthounds).

Kohnke, J. *Veterinary Advice for
Greyhound Owners.*
Ring Press Books Ltd.,
Hertfordshire, England. 1994.

Lackey, Sue. *Greyhounds in
America, Vol. 1.* Greyhound
Club of America. 1988.
(Excellent account of AKC
greyhounds; out of print).

Miller, Constance O.
*Gazehounds: The Search for
Truth.* Hoflin Publishing,
Wheat Ridge, CO. 1988.
(History of all sighthounds).

Rolins, A. *All About the
Greyhound.* Rigby Publishers,
Willoughby, NSW 2068,
Australia. 1982.

Video

Greyhound #VVT411
The American Kennel Club
Attn: Video Fulfillment
5580 Centerview Drive #200
Raleigh, NC 27606
(919) 233-9780

Soundness Examination of the
    Racing Greyhound
James C. Gannon
available from the NGA
P.O. Box 543
Abilene, KS 67410
(913) 263-4660

Index

Abuse, 15
Acepromazine, 58
Adoption, 10–11, 15, 18
Age, 14, 17
Aggression, 83
Agility, 91
Air travel, 38
American Kennel Club (AKC),
   10, 17–18, 75, 93, 101
Allergies, 44, 46–47
American Association of Feed
   Control Officers
   (AAFCO), 41
American Boarding Kennel
   Association (ABKA), 38,
   101
American Sighthound Field
   Association (ASFA), 75
Anal sacs, 65
Anesthesia, 55, 57–58
Antifreeze, 26
Appetite, changes in, 55
Arthritis, 54
Artificial respiration, 62–63
Aspirin, 54, 71

Bald thigh syndrome, 47, 57
Barbiturates, 57
Barking, 83
Bathing, 46
Bedding, 22, 24
Begging, 80–81
Behavior, 20
Benadryl, 37
Biting, 83
Bleeding, 63
Bloating, 45, 58, 62, 64
Blood:
   donors, 57
   pressure, 57
   type, 57
Boarding, 38, 55
Body language, 35, 66
Breathing difficulties, 62–63
Breeding, 19
Bulldog, 7
Burns, 63

Cages, 24, 30–31, 38
Calluses, 47
Cars, 22, 28, 38
Cataracts, 55
Cats, 32–33, 36, 69, 77, 83
Champion (AKC), 97
Chewing, 25, 28, 82
Chilblains, 51
Children, 20–22, 68
Chocolate, 26, 44
Class (racing), 13
Coat, 22, 43, 46
Collar, 23, 81, 84
Color, 7, 18, 29, 95–96
   vision, 34
"Come," 73, 85–86
Commands, 78
Conditioning, 67–69
Convulsions, 63
Coughing, 61, 64
Coursing, 6–8, 74–77
Cruciate ligament, 55, 71
Cushing's syndrome, 55

Dandruff, 46, 97
Dangers, 26–28, 69, 72–74, 84
Deer, 72
Dental care, 52–54, 55
Destructive behavior, 82
Dewclaws, 50
Diabetes, 65
Diarrhea, 43, 55, 65
Diatomaceous earth, 47
Dogs (other), 32, 71–72, 83
Dominance, 83
Doors, 26–27
"Down," 86–87
Drowning, 62–63

Ears, 34, 37, 50–51, 54, 68
Electrical shock, 63
Emergencies, 62–63
Energy, 20
Erlichiosis, 50
Esophageal achalasia, 58, 64
Euthanasia, 99
Exercise, 55, 67–69

Expenses, 12, 17, 20
Eye disorders, 65–66
Eyes, 54

Facial expression, 34–35
Fat (in food), 43, 65
Fat ratio (of body), 57
Fearfulness, 83
Feeding, 41–45
Feet, 33, 70
Fences, 27
Fighting, 20, 83
First aid kit, 62
Flea collars, 47–48
Fleas, 46–50
Forest Laws, 7
Fractures, 71
Furniture, 22, 31

Galloping, 9, 11
Games, 73
Gastric dilation torsion, 45, 58,
   62, 64
Genetics, 95–96
Gray color, 7, 96
Greyhound Club of America,
   18–19, 87, 101
Greyhound Hall of Fame, 14
Grooming, 46

Hair, 43, 46
Hair loss, 46–47
Hearing, 34, 55
Heart:
   disease, 43, 55, 64
   rate, 57
   size, 57
Heartworm, 61
Heat, 60, 76
Heatstroke, 33, 62, 68
Heel, 86–87
Hereditary disorders, 11, 58
History, 6–11
Hounds, 20
Housebreaking, 24, 28–29,
   31–32
House soiling, 82–83

Immunity, 55, 60
Impetigo, 47
Indefinite Listing Privilege
    number (ILP number), 75
Infection, 54, 65
Injuries, 18, 22, 27, 70–71, 76
Insect Growth Regulators (IGR),
    48–49
Insects, 37
Intestinal parasites, 60–61
Itching, 46–47

Jogging, 68–69
Jumping, 27
Jumping up, 83

Kennel cough, 61, 64
Kidney disease, 43, 55, 65

Leash, 23
Leash training, 86
License tags, 23, 39
Limping, 55, 66, 70–71
Longevity, 11, 17
Lost dog, 39
Lumps, 54
Lure-coursing, 74–77
Lure training, 12–13
Lyme disease, 50

Mange, 50
Matches, 97
Meat, 34, 42–43
Medications, 59
Metabolism, 44, 55
Microchip, 39, 101
Motels, 38
Muzzles, 13–14, 16, 32

Nails, 50–51, 70
Name, 29
Nasal discharge, 55
National Greyhound Association
    (NGA), 9–10, 15, 17–18, 33
National Open Field Coursing
    Association (NOFCA), 74
Numbers, 10, 15–16

Obedience, 22, 78–88, 90–91
    classes, 87–88

trials, 90–91
Odor, 22, 54
Older dogs, 43–44, 65, 83
Olfaction, 34, 91
Open field coursing, 74
Osteosarcoma, 55, 58, 66

Pads, 33, 68, 70, 76–77
Pain, 37, 70–71
Pannus, 66
Pen, 24, 28
Pesticides, 47–50
Pet quality, 18–19
Pet sitter, 38–39
Pets (other), 32
Physiology, 57–58
Pills, 59
Poisoning, 63
Poison plants, 27
Pole lure, 13, 75
Popularity, 10
Pressure points, 63
Prostate, 65
Protein, 43
Puppies, 12, 17

Rabbits, 8–9, 13, 32, 74
Race training, 12–13
Racing, 9, 12–13, 16, 76
Registration, 75–76, 96,
    101

Safety, 26–28, 69, 72–74, 84
Saluki, 6–7
Senses, 34
Separation anxiety, 32,
    82–83
Shampoo, 46
Shock, 62
Showing, 10–11, 19, 96–97
Sighthound, 7, 34, 74, 91
"Sit," 79, 81, 84
Size, 17, 22
Skin, 55
    problems, 66
Smell, 22, 34, 54
Snakebites, 63
Speed, 9, 14, 18
Stairs, 31–32
Standard (AKC), 93–96

"Stay," 84–85
Stings, 37
Submission, 35, 82
Swimming, 27–28, 67

Tail, 22, 26, 28, 35, 66
Tapeworm, 59, 61
Taste, 34, 43
Tattoo, 14, 39
Teeth, 52–55
Temperament, 20–22
Temperature:
    internal, 59, 62
    ambient, 33, 76
Therapy dog, 98
Thirst, increased, 65
Thyroid, 47, 57
Ticks, 50
Titles, 75, 90–92, 97
Toes, 70–71
Tongue, 33, 60
Toys, 25
Trachea, collapsed, 64
Tracking, 91
Training, 22, 31–32, 78–88
Travel, 37–38, 42
Tricks, 89
Tumor, 55, 66
Tying, 26

Urinary tract, 65
Urinary incontinence, 65
Urination:
    increased, 55, 65
    painful, 65

Vaccinations, 59–60
Veterinarian, 59, 71
Vision, 34, 55
Vomiting, 64–65

Walking, 67–68
Waste disposal, 25, 38
Watchdog, 22
Weather, 33
Weight, 22, 44
    change, 55
Worms, 60–61, 64–65
    medications, 48, 61
Wounds, 63